Church and Empire

Church and Empire

Detailing Theological Musings

Y. T. Vinayaraj

CWI

Christian World Imprints

First Published in 2019 by

Christian World Imprints
Christian Publishing & Books from India
C-3, Shop No. 14, Ground Floor
Wazirpur Industrial Area, **Delhi-110052**
cwidelhi2017@gmail.com
www.ChristianWorldImprints.com
Phone: +91 11 41526079

ISBN: 978-93-5148-391-5 (HB)
ISBN: 978-93-5148-399-1 (PB)

Printed in India.

Dedicated to my father
A.R. Yehu

Contents

Foreword

I am very happy that Rev. Dr. Y. T. Vinayaraj has published these papers on Church and Empire, which he had formerly presented at national and international seminars, now in the form of a book. It is clear that these studies focus on the life and witness of the faith community in the context of the Empire. The author calls for a radical ecclesiology of the excluded and the unqualified, and challenges the traditional notions of ecumenism and ecclesia. He advocates for a contextual ecclesiology that seriously considers new strategies of mission and ministry in India and identifies the greatest challenges of the church in the contemporary world. The prevailing notion of ecumenism is being questioned and a search for a relevant theology of ecumenism in the context of empire is made. The presentations also highlight the dangers of ecumenism based on the imperial logic of 'oneness' and re-defines ecumenism as a radical ontology of the multitude and common wealth in the context of empire.

Another major theme in this volume is the messianic vocation of the church which is to be grounded on anti imperial eschatology that takes seriously the present moment in relation to end-time and eternity. These presentations will surely enable the theological academia to re-imagine ecumenism and church in a meaningful way. Another theme expounded in this volume is Christian Mission in the

'Postcolonial World'. In this context, the nexus between Christianity and Empire, theology and politics is exposed and Christian theology and mission rooted in the subaltern ethical and religious epistemologies (that seriously considers Ambedkar's understanding on religion and his critique on Christianity) is advocated.

There is also an attempt to delimit the limitations of popularly accepted atonement theories and the readers are encouraged to re-imagine the biopolitics of the crucified as the redemptive act of resistance of the tortured bodies. This has great significance in the contemporary context of empire. Theology of cross is explained as story about God's solidarity with the oppressed that led Jesus Christ to the death on the cross. Participation of the faith community in the death and resurrection of Jesus Christ event becomes an act of promise of hope in the contemporary world of violence.

The author challenges certain theological and philosophical notions of God and other in the human relationship and in the christian ethics, and proposes a method that recognizes the contemporary epistemological context of multi-disciplinarity by developing a radical political ontology and materialist theology. These articles identify the role of the theological academia and the church as to formulate biblical hermeneutics, liturgical discourses and ministerial models that will enable them to listen to the voice of the silenced by re-articulating their own ontology. I am sure that these theological and philosophical engagements on the theme church and empire will definitely enrich the theological academia and the faith community in India.

Rev. Dr. Prakash K. George
Principal
Mar Thoma Theological Seminary, Kottayam
Chairperson, Academic Council
The Senate of Serampore College (University), Kolkata

Acknowledgements

This book is a collection of essays and talks in various seminars and conferences on the theme church and empire. It is compiled and published in the conviction that the church has come to a time when it cannot but encounter empire from within and without to witness the crucified Christ. Christ has been crucified not because of the imperial persecution of Christians; rather, because of his radical encounter with the logic of Roman imperialism that enslaved the weak and killed the slaves. The empire upholds its power by legitimizing its right to kill the slaves. The act of crucifixion still remains in history as the symbol of the resistance of the weak against the necropolitics of the empire. The resurrection of Jesus, on the other hand, provides hope for the tortured and the crucified by reiterating the eschatological victory of the 'outlaw justice.'

Christian theology cannot but be political in its content as it stems out of Jesus' crucifixion and resurrection in history. Christian theology is always a political theology. It invokes the church and society to be de-imperialized and provokes it to become the ardent advocate of social democracy and justice. Thus, theology has to be the theology of de-imperialization and de-colonization. The talks and presentations are formulated out of such a theological conviction and foundation. Some of these presentations are already published in various publications and I am grateful to the concerned editors and publishers. I am indebted to many who have enriched me with new ideas and encouraged me with their love. I want to thank all my friends and colleagues at the Mar Thoma Theological Seminary, Kottayam where I have been fortunate and privileged to have meaningful conversations.

I am extremely grateful to Rev. Dr. Prakash K. George, the principal, Mar Thoma Theological Seminary, Kottayam, who has been gracious enough to write a meaningful foreword to this book. I am thankful to Anshul Kanda, the editorial head, Christian World Imprints for the willingness to publish this book. I want to thank Ani Alex Kurian for reading the manuscript. Finally I want to thank my family for their love and support–especially my wife Smitha and my children Emil and Alen as well as my mother, Thabeetha. This book is dedicated to my father, A.R. Yehu who not only gave me the gift of life but was also my first teacher.

1

Re-Claiming Ecclesia in the Context of Empire*

Introduction

The honorable Synod of the Church of South India is to be acknowledged and appreciated for promoting new theological discourses for the edification and the ministry of the church in India. Of course, no one can deny or disregard the contributions of this church and its theologians in the process of envisaging contextual and significant doctrinal engagements in this country. Now, the effort to re-imagine ecclesiology is going to be yet another significant mark in the contextual theological thinking in this country as it is facing new challenges of neo-liberal economy, culture, and spirituality. In the crucial context of marginalization and destitution, as the concept note of this consultation rightly says, it is the high time for the Indian

---

* This essay is the abstract of the talk given at the National Consultation on "Border-less Church" organized by the Church of South India at CSI Headquarters Chennai on October 20, 2018.

Church to re-construct its ontology (being and becoming), theology (and epistemology), and spirituality (both liturgy and politics) in favour of the victims and the excluded.

The quest for a borderless church is to make the Church open and inclusive. However, the site of the border is no more a space of hospitality and alterity today. Rather, it has become the site of estrangement, hatred, and violence. The border, whether it is in terms of nationality, re(li)gion, caste or gender, is to be the site of welcoming and conviviality as it envisages a radical space (and time) of deconstruction and reconstruction. It is the site of the divine epiphany where we reconcile, forgive, and trans-form each other for a new being, becoming and belonging. It is the eschatological space and messianic time where we de-other 'the other' and de-self 'the self.' Just as the marginal space of the Cross of Jesus Christ, the border is the site of shared pain and the celebrated hope. Russell Chandran once said, the crucifixion and the resurrection are not two separate events; rather they are concurrent events—the fragments of the Christ Event that determine the redemption of all (Chandran: 1985). We need a theology of border in the crucial context of hatred, violence, violation and segregation that invokes us to envisage a borderless church—an inclusive community of Christ/ Christic community. Church as a borderless community should not be a homogenous community; rather, it is to be a 'community of communities,' as Dyanchand Carr alludes always (Carr: 2007).

Rethinking the Church as a borderless community needs to be theologized with caution in the very particular context of empire. The empire also claims to be an open-global community. It is also a borderless –'imagined community' of Market that operates itself within the logic of neo-liberal economy and culture. Being the ideology of destitution, the claim of the empire to be an 'inclusive' community is to be interrogated and resisted. It is inclusive and at the same time, it is exclusive. The Italian philosopher Giorgio Agamben calls this political dilemma 'the state of exception', in order to expose the inherent problem of inside and outside—ontology and politics in the concept of empire. Thus, the quest for an open Church in the context of empire demands a radical ecclesiology of the excluded and the unqualified to be in the 'main-stream.'

Another important issue is all about the question of the de-imperialization of the Church. Assuming the status of the empire, the Church in history has offered the theologies of mission and ministry without de-imperializing its own ontology (being and becoming). Being the structure of patriarchy and hierarchy, many a time in history, the Church has claimed its authority and power in terms of administration, but not in ministry. It is here, we realize the imperative to differentiate the logic of empire and Ecclesia as they differ in their logic of inclusivity and borderless-ness. This paper tries to delineate the epistemological difference between the terms—empire and Ecclesia and thereby offer a constructive proposal for a contemporary ecclesiology, which re-defines Church as a de-imperialized being and becoming. It explores the possibility of envisaging new strategies of mission and ministry in India by initiating significant and relevant theological discourses.

Empire and Ecclesia: Deconstructing the History of an Illegitimate Alliance

Joerg Rieger, while analyzing the relationship between the Church and empire, offers two different responses (Rieger, 2007: 9). On one side, he argues that early Christianity was a critique of the Roman Empire, which constituted the context of early Christianity. The Jesus' movement and the apostolic traditions envisaged counter imperial communities that denied the imperial practices of exclusion and marginalization. At the same time, Rieger points out that Christianity after the Constantine era assumed a hierarchical/ imperial structure. The early ecumenical councils convened by the emperors signify the involvement of imperial forces in the formulation of Christian doctrines and dogmatics. It is really exciting to read Giorgio Agamben, when he investigates the context of the emergence of the theology of *oikoumene* (economic trinity) in the patristic period over against the totalitarianism of the Constantine political power (Agamben, 2011: 50). Thus, the relationship between the empire and the Church has always been apprehensive and cryptic. This is true as we go through the historical periods of the crusades and the modern mission strategies of the Western Church colluded with European colonialism.

Exposing the trajectory of the conviviality between the Church and the empire, Elizabeth Schussler Fiorenza offers a theological treatise on anti-imperial ecclesiology in her incredible work—*The Power of the Word: Scripture and the Rhetoric of Empire*. In this book, Fiorenza speaks about Church as a political space— "the radial democracy of equals" (Fiorenza: 2007). The radical democracy of Fiorenza is the *ekklesia of wo/men,* which offers the language and space for the imagination to develop a public religious discourse, "wherein justice, participation, difference, freedom, equality, and solidarity set the ethical conditions" (Hernandez, 1997: 31). Fiorenza, in contradiction to the kyriarchal model of the empire, defines the Church as a radical political space where the logic of domination and subordination is denied, and equality and justice for all is affirmed. Fiorenza articulates Christian community—Church as the radical democratic assembly of all, the *cosmopolis* of God's very different peoples (Fiorenza, 2001: 56).

Alluding to Paul, Alain Badiou signifies the Pauline theology of the Christ-Event as the "counter-community of resistance" to envisage a radical ecclesiology in the emerging context of the empire (Badiou: 2003). Richard Horsley's *Paul and Empire* and *Paul and Politics* offer a convincing case of defining Church as an anti-imperial imagination (Horsley: 1997). In his *Insurrection of the Crucified,* Theodore W. Jennings Jr. provides another hermeneutical approach for envisaging the Church as an anti-imperial community (Jennings: 2003). Engaging with Michael Hardt and Antonio Negri, Joerg Rieger and Kwok Pui-lan embark on an "Ecclesia of the Multitude," in their well-read book *Occupy Religion: Theology of the Multitude.* According to them, the Church of the Multitude is the "gathering of diverse people, and it orients them toward service in the world, particularly toward the least among us" (Rieger & Pui-lan: 2011). Here, the empire is envisaged as the hegemonic logic of neo-liberal capitalism, which legitimizes the ideology of exclusion, the politics of refugization, and the economy of destitution. For them, the Church as an anti-imperial imagination, which deconstructs its hierarchical ontology and other-centered *diakonia,* envisages a radical democratic community of justice and equality for all. The task before the Church in the context of the empire is to be the Church of the Multitude.

Church as the Coming Community: Giorgio Agamben

It is Giorgio Agamben, the Italian philosopher/theologian, who rightly analyzes and exposes the imperial inheritance of the Church in the post-Constantine period (Agamben, 2011: 104). Alluding to Paul, Agamben contends that by claiming itself as the kingdom of God or the divinely legitimized empire, the Church denied its call (*klesis*) to be *paroikousa* (sojourner) and ended up as *katoikein* (to dwell like an empire). When the Church becomes a sovereign power of rule and its liturgies become the celebration of the sovereign God, the calling of the Church is nullified and reversed. Engaging with the Pauline corpus, Giorgio Agamben offers an extended discussion on the "calling" (*kletos)* of the Church. It is a calling that calls back or revokes every other vocation. According to Agamben, the calling of the Church is a call for a messianic vocation that revokes all other vocations in the context of the reign of the emperor. For him, the Church is a "messianic community" that lives in messianic time (Agamben, 1993: 1-2). Messianic time, as it is well explained in the Pauline corpus, is the time that remains—the time in-between the ascension and *parousia*. It is the time that remains in-between the Church and kingdom of God—the time the *ekklesia* takes to come to its end. End time, thus is not a futuristic time; rather, it is a qualitative "now"—the time of redemption within the present time (Agamben, 2005: 6-7). Agamben defines Church as a "coming community" that locates itself in a "state of exception"—the site of the marginalized and the excluded and thereby envisages political ontology of the crucified.

By "the coming community" or "the community that comes", Agamben means a community of those who have no community. It is a community of people who are being "excluded in" or "included out" in the sovereign political paradigm. It is a community that cannot be co-opted by totalitarian forces. Or it is a community where the sovereign law is being inactivated. It is the community of the de-imperialized subjectivities. Agamben finds this sense of inoperability of the logic of the empire in the kenotic act of Christ on the Cross.

First and foremost, the Cross signifies the inoperability of the biopolitics of sovereignty and offers a radical politics of community by replacing himself on the cross in the place of a political victim in the Roman imperial context. In his reading on Paul, Agamben comments that the calling of the Church is to "enslave" itself to this Messiah who becomes weak for the most wretched of the earth (Agamben, 2012: 13-14). For Agamben, Church is called to be the ontology of the marginalized, the tortured—the Multitude.

The Church as a "coming community" embodies the messianic politics through which it takes a turn from liturgy to politics. It is through messianic politics that the Church becomes part of the democratic process that challenges the contemporary socio-political and economic sovereign powers. It is through messianic politics that the Church re-invents its ontology in relation to "social ontology." Defining politics as a "social ontology," Chantal Mouffe says that "the political cannot be restricted to a certain type of institution, or envisioned as constituting a specific sphere or level of society. It must be conceived as a dimension that is inherent to every human society and that determines our very ontological condition (Mouffe, 2005: 3)." Church as a "coming community" envisages a "social ontology" that challenges the exclusionary practices of the sovereign power and embodies the agonistic politics of the excluded and exempted in our democratic process. It is the *messianic politics* that signifies the Church in the contemporary socio-economic and political context of the empire. It is the messianic politics that makes redemption happen in the everyday life of the people.

Church as New Humanity: M. M. Thomas

Among Indian Christian theologians, it was M. M. Thomas who proposed an authentic political ecclesiology in the Indian context. Responding to the state of emergency declared at the midnight of June 25-26, 1975, Thomas said: "It is nothing but the onslaught on democracy and a betrayal of the nation." Thomas contended that the effort to quell people's revolts for the sake of internal peace, economic progress, and self-reliance through a state of emergency was nothing but the repudiation of all human rights envisaged by a welfare state and its democracy. Thomas envisages a participatory democracy where the sovereign power of the state is nullified and the rights of the marginalized are celebrated. Redefining the Church as the sign of the secular Koinonia and New Humanity, Thomas envisions radical ecclesiology as it destabilizes the logic of the empire within (Vinayaraj, 2017: 119).

Thomas' theology of state and democracy is founded on his theology of the Cross. According to Thomas, Jesus' cross is a protest against the sovereignty of the Roman Empire and the act of crucifixion was to nullify its logic of domination and marginalization. Replacing a political victim on the cross, Jesus exemplified his political solidarity and identification. Jesus' cross signifies the end of the totalitarian power and the beginning of a new community—the kingdom community—a universal community where there are no dichotomies. In the new community, "there is no longer any distinction between Gentiles and Jews, circumcised and uncircumcised, barbarians, savages, slaves and free; but Christ is all and in all" (Col. 3:11). The new human community is constituted as a single body—the body of the crucified God in history. The crucified body of Christ is not a new thing; rather it is the body of the slain Lamb from the creation of the world and it continues to be slain till the end of the world, fighting against the totalitarian forces of powers. The mark of crucifixion continues to be the sign of the suffering struggle of God against the principalities and powers till the end of the world. The mission of the Church today is to embody this mark of crucifixion and to reconstitute its ontology in solidarity with the victims of the world.

According to Thomas, the Church is entrusted with a prophetic *diakonia* to discharge its duty based on the servanthood exemplified by the crucified God. Thomas writes: "The church in India is called to proclaim the gospel of the crucified and risen Christ as the source of redemption of all spiritualities underlying religion as well as ideologies, and to demonstrate the Koinonia in Christ around the Eucharist as the nucleus of a movement of the larger Koinonia in Christ uniting peoples of diverse religions, ideologies and cultures—as well as the cosmos with its bio-diversity" (Thomas, 1995: 15). Based on his theology of the Cross, M. M. Thomas explains the features of the mission of the church in India: (1) the calling of the church is to resist the idolatry of power and wealth and other gods of death in India's collective life, (2) to be in solidarity with the poor and the oppressed in their struggle for justice, and (3) to give up communal self-interest and self-identity for the sake of creating in India a secular national community in the midst of India's religious and ideological pluralism through manifesting a fellowship in Christ, transcending class, caste, ethnic and religious communal divisions (Thomas, 1990: 11).

Thomas' theology of humanization, through which he upholds an anti-imperial ecclesiology and missiology, makes him very significant and relevant. Thomas finds the foundation for his eschatological anthropology in the theology of the Spirit who raised Jesus from the dead as the first fruits of the New Creation. Thomas' hope in the future of humanity is incorporated in his understanding of the Risen Christ and His coming. He cites Paul: "We await a Saviour, the Lord Jesus Christ who will change our lowly body to be like his glorious body, by the power which enables him even to subject all to himself" (Phil. 3: 20-21). By becoming the tortured body of Christ, the Church is being composed and constituted as an open community of all to resist the logic of the empire theologically, liturgically, and hermeneutically. According to Thomas, it is this call and the composition of the Church to be and become a messianic community only that signifies its relevance in the contemporary context of Empire.

Making Church the Messianic Community Today

Let me bring some painful stories here from Kerala. Recently there raised a nun was a case of abuse against a Bishop. Some nuns connected with the abused sisters awere on hunger strike demanding the arrest of the accused Bishop. However, the church that the Bishop belongs to and the other established churches are elther observing silence or supporting the accured indirectly. The public in India is of the opinion that the illegitimate alliance of the church with the ruling government try to disrupt the police enquiry and save the acaused. It is a clear example where the established churches, in alliance with the power-centers, deny justice to the victim, particularly a victim who belongs to the body of the church. This is one among many cases as we see the illegitimate alliance between the church and empire, through which it excludes the poor and the weak.

Generally speaking, the empire in India today takes many forms of hegemony in terms of cultural, economic, political, and religious realms. The logic of empire intrudes into the very aspect of human life. It denies our rights to food, clothing, study and belief. There is no security for a Dalit, woman, or transgender in the public spaces. Religion has become the ideology of hatred. The economy of the empire is nothing but the "economy of suicide" that demands the farmers to sacrifice their life for development. The cultural, religious, and linguistic minorities are in anxiety and fear. Dalits are being termed "anti-nationals." The people who stand for human rights are being killed. Intolerance constitutes the public life. On the other hand, the national elite, the multinational corporations, the international nuclear regimes, find home in India. The notions of state, democracy and the people are being transformed in favour of the global Capitalism. The Church in India finds difficulty to respond to this scenario. The silence of the churches is regarded as the conspiracy for the empire.

The challenge before the Church in India today is not just to preach about its inherited salvation to the world around; rather, it is to experience the fragments of salvation in this world by becoming the ontology of the weak. The challenge before the Church is to be the Church of the crucified people. As Agamben opines, it is an act of retreat for the Church to "inoperate" its inherent juridical structure and to become a "coming community"—a community that is a community of those who have no community. By becoming the messianic community of the weak, it engages critically with the exploitative systems of our society to make it just and egalitarian. Radical ecclesiology is a call within the call of the Church (*klesis*) to become the "weak church" of the Crucified God by becoming the body of the crucified people "now". Agamben exhorts that the task of the Church today is to find its eschatological moment—the moment when it becomes the open church of all: "Living in this time, experiencing this time, is thus not something that the Church can choose, or choose not, to do. It is only in this time that there is a Church at all" (Agamben, 2012: 13).

References

Adriana Hernandez, *Pedagogy, Democracy, and Feminism: Rethinking the Public Sphere* (New York: State University of New York Press, 1997).

Alain Badiou, *Saint Paul: The Foundation of Universalism* (Stanford: Stanford University Press, 2003).

Chantal Mouffe, *The Return of the Political* (New York: Verso, 2005).

Elizabeth Schussler Fiorenza, *The Power of the Word: Scripture and the Rhetoric of Empire* (Minneapolis: Fortress Press, 2007).

Giorgio Agamben, *The Coming Community* (Minneapolis: University of Minnesota Press, 1993).

Giorgio Agamben, *The Church and the Kingdom* (London, New York, Calcutta: Seagull Books, 2003).

Giorgio Agamben, *The Time That Remains: A Commentary on the Letter to the Romans* (Stanford, CA: Stanford University Press, 2005).

Giorgio Agamben, *The Kingdom and Glory: For a Theological Genealogy of Economy and Government* (Stanford: Stanford University Press, 2011).

Joerg Rieger & Kwok Pui-lan, *Occupy Religion: Theology of the Multitude* (New York & UK: Rowan & Litlefield Publishers, 2012).

M. M. Thomas, "The Church in India—Witness to the Meaning of the Cross Today," in *Future of the Church in India*, ed. Aruna Gnanadason (Nagpur: NCCI, 1990).

M. M. Thomas, *A Diaconal Approach to Indian Ecclesiology* (Rome & Tiruvalla: CIIS & CSS, 1995).

Richard Horsley, ed., *Paul and Empire: Religion and Power in Roman Imperial Society* (Harrisburg, P.A: Trinity Press, 1997).

Theodore Jennings W, *The Insurrection of the Crucified: The "Gospel of Mark" as Theological Manifesto* (Chicago, IL: exploration Press, 2003).

Y. T. Vinayaraj, *Theology after Hardt & Negri: Empire, Church and Multitude* (Delhi: ISPCK, 2017).

2

Re-Claiming Ecumenism in the Context of Empire*

Introduction

Etymologically speaking, the Greek word *oikoumene,* which generally means "the whole inhabited world," out of which the notion of Ecumenism has been derived, was implied to Roman Empire in the first century BCE. Both in biblical and ecclesiastical traditions the word *oikoumene* was used to signify the political meaning of the Roman Empire. Biblical scholars argue that the word *oikoumene* in both Testaments generally signifies the imperial rule that entails God's judgment and trial. They hardly find any biblical references that *oikoumene* signifies God's creation (Rossing, 2013: 174-176). In the 4th and 5th centuries, *oikoumene* was used to denote the Christian councils convoked by the emperors. In this period, *oikoumene* was used to signify the imperial authority and legitimacy of the decisions

---

* Paper Presented at the Congress of Asian Theologians (CATS-VIII) on 18-22, April 2016 at Cochin.

taken by the early church councils. On the other hand, the modern Ecumenical Movement used this term in the twentieth century to imply the global unity of churches and later to the wider ecumenism—the unity of whole creation. However, alluding to Barbara Rossing, the well-known Lutheran biblical scholar, who exposes the etymological conviviality between Ecumenism and Empire, this essay asks whether the contemporary theology of Ecumenism repudiates the imperial trajectory of *oikoumene.* If then how?

Furthermore, the Patristic notion of *oikonomia* (economic trinity) which later became the philosophical/theological foundation for Ecumenism offered a 'mysterious unity' between God and the creation. The Patristic notion of *oikonomia* was originally conceptualized against the monotheism of the Emperor Constantine. *Oikoumene* affirms the equivocity—the absolute difference—between the Creator and the creation. Here, God is sovereign and the creation is connected to divine as the "exterior other.' The creation—the 'other' is accommodated within the ontology of God (Being of God) through the act of salvation. The contemporary philosophers and postcolonial theologians interrogate this notion of *oikonomia* (economy of life) for legitimizing an imperial logic of 'Oneness' and locating 'creation' as the 'exterior other.' Like *oikonomia,* the contemporary notion of empire–the post capitalized economy and politics also offers an 'enclosed ontology', by which it legitimizes an imperial logic of 'Oneness.' Hence, this essay asks whether the theology of Ecumenism disavows the imperial logic of 'Oneness' and affirms 'multiplicity' and 'manyness.'

Engaging with post-Continental and post colonial theological discourses, this essay asks: (1) What would be a relevant theology of Ecumenism in the contemporary context of empire? (2) If Ecumenism denies the unitarian logic of empire, then how does it define the life in common? In other words, how does the unity perception of Ecumenism differ from the imperial logic of 'Oneness'? This distinction is very crucial for the re-imagination of ecumenism and church today. Thus, this essay offers a constructive proposal for re-imagining Ecumenism and Ecclesiology today. It has three major sections; the first section exposes the nuances involved in the etymological conviviality between empire and Ecumenism as they are derived from the same root word *oikoumene* in both biblical and Roman literature. The second section delineates the contemporary political meaning of the empire and its hegemonic logic of 'Oneness' as it is exposed by Antonio Negri and Michael Hardt. Signifying their concepts of *multitude* and *commonwealth*, the third section offers a radical theology of Ecumenism and Ecclesiology in the contemporary context of empire.

Ecumenism and Empire: The Etymological Paradox

In the first century BCE, the word *oikoumene* was used as a synonym for the Roman Empire. Barbara Rossing is of the opinion that 'in relation with the Roman political conquests of lands and peoples, *oikoumene* claimed not only the ends of the world in a geographical sense but also in a political sense, as the ends of Roman imperial sway' (Rossing, 2013: 174). Claude Nicolet supports this argument and contends that the Roman Empire and its geographical knowledge developed hand in hand, as evidenced in the use of the Greek word *oikoumene* (Nicolet, 1991: 174). In that period, the Romans were called "lords of the oikoumene" (*kyrioi tes oikoumenes*). Ancient authors such as Josephus use the term *oikoumene* for the imperial propaganda and even call Romans as the "recruited inhabitants" of the *oikoumene* from the uninhabited world (*aoiketou*). In this sense, *oikoumene* points to the geographical area that is controlled by the Roman government and not the whole inhabited earth.

Biblical literature also followed this notion and defined *oikoumene* as the Roman Empire. Delineating it, Barbara Rossing argues that in the Septuagint, *oikoumene* is used to denote the Roman Empire—an empire that must come to an end. The Roman Empire, as she explains in the book of Revelation, is nothing but a hegemonic rule that requires a trial or judgment (Rossing, 2013: 176). She writes: "In light of the book's [the book of Revelation] overall anti-Roman polemic, the hour of trial that is coming upon the whole *oikoumene* in Rev. 3:10 should be read not so much as a general eschatological tribulation that will come upon the earth, but more pointedly as the trial or judgment that God will bring upon the entire Roman Empire and on all those who benefit from Rome's injustice" (Rossing, 2013: 177). Though there are some parallel references on *oikoumene* and earth (*ge*), for e.g., Psalm 18, the word *oikoumene* in the biblical literature predominantly refers to the Roman imperial world. Rossing is of the opinion that both in Old Testament and New Testament there is no such clear connotation for *oikoumene* as God's creation. Rather it connotes a pagan rule that anticipates the divine judgment and trial.

In the 4th and 5th centuries, *oikoumene* was used to denote the ecumenical councils. The early Christian councils were convoked by emperors who summoned the bishops, paid their expenses, and gave their decisions binding force. These councils were called 'ecumenical' since the bishops represented the world. Another significant term that is to be noted in this Patristic tradition is *oikonomia* (economic trinity). Early church fathers defined the salvific act of God on the basis of 'economic trinity' through which they affirmed the sovereignty of God and God's external (mysterious) connection with creation. In order to challenge the monotheistic tradition of Constantine while affirming the equivocity (the absolute difference) between Creator and Creation, the early church fathers found refuge in this concept of 'economic trinity.' Giorgio Agamben, in his critical analysis, contends that through this theological notion, the early church was able to accommodate the creation within the divine program of salvation as its 'exterior other' (Agamben, 2011: 50-51). The other is mysteriously (*sacramentum*) accommodated within as the 'exterior other' and thus the sovereignty of the 'transcendental Other—wholly Other—God is affirmed.

On the contrary, the Ecumenical Movement defined *oikoumene* as God's *oikos* (household) with the vision of global justice and peace. Following the theological notion of *basileia* (kingdom of God), the Ecumenical Movement signified *oikoumene* as the Christian vision of a just-community and eco-justice. Differentiating the unitarian logic of globalization with the ecumenical vision of plurality and diversity, the WCC Harare assembly used two categories: "*oikoumene* of domination' and the other is "the *oikoumene* of faith and solidarity" (Kessler, 1998). K.C. Abraham calls this '*oikoumene* of solidarity' 'liberative ecumenism'–a common platform for all religions to come together and struggle for justice and human liberation (Abraham, 1993: 174). The problem that we face here is that neither the biblical tradition nor the ecclesiastical tradition gives substantiate philosophical/ theological foundation for this "oikoumene of solidarity" unless we read the scripture with new hermeneutical tools. How do we explain this 'oikoumene of solidarity' disavowing the imperil logic of unity? Even the notion of the kingdom of God replicates the nuances of the Empire! How does ecumenism substantiate multiplicity and alterity in social organization and imagination? Does this ecumenism re-instate the notion of the sovereign God who legitimizes the ontology of the empire? This essay tries to attend some of these questions by bringing in the contemporary political concepts like *multitude* and *commonwealth* in our discussion in order to re-claim Ecumenism today as we envision 'a life in common' over against the logic of Empire.

Multitude and Commonwealth: 'Living in Common'

Antonio Negri, the Italian philosopher (with Michael Hardt) offers a detailed discussion on the contemporary project of empire (Negri & Hardt, 2004). Their notion of empire is not a military—imperial regime like the Roman Empire or the American Empire. Negri opines that such forms of imperialism are over. For Hardt and Negri, the empire signifies a post-globalized human condition where we see the free flow of capital, information, and technology. Negri and Hardt describe it: "the empire is an imaginative geography of globalization of world space, where boundless flow of capital, labour and information transcend the older imperialist order and yet at the same time plant the seeds of the destruction and transformation of the empire" (Negri & Hardt, 2004: 137). The empire has no territorial center of power and does not rely on any territorial boundaries. It is a global net-work of power. As Negri explains, the empire "is a decentered and deterritorializing apparatus of rule that progressively incorporates the entire global realm within its open, expanding frontiers" (Negri & Hardt, 2004: xiii). "The empire is materializing before our eyes.... Along with global order, a new logic of structure and rule—in short a new form of sovereignty" (Negri & Hardt, 2004: xiii).

The empire proposes a sovereign political power at the center of the global economy that legitimizes the exclusion of the majority.

The migrants, the refugees, the traditional workers, the indigenous people, weaker sections and the farmers become excluded from the sovereign global market economy. They live at the margins of global economy. This site of marginality is not outside of the global economic ontology (empire); rather it is the marginality that reinstates the sovereign ontology of the empire. Any resistance to the empire re-instating this centrality-marginality dialectical Oneness will not help us to envision a radical democracy. The resistances that do not de-marginalize the margin and de-centralize the center will ultimately substantiate the sovereign ontology of the empire. That is what we see in the case of terrorism. As Negri rightly points out, terrorism is not to deny the empire but to control the empire. Thus, resistances that aim to nullify the logic of empire should re-imagine democracy in terms of multiplicity and politics in terms of multitude.

On the more, the sovereignty of this global economy and the exclusion of the majority is theologically legitimized by the notion of sovereign God which is foundational for the theology of global capitalism. In this theology, the sovereign God is the transcendent God as in the case of the transcendent capital. However, it is a charity oriented God who stretches out His hands for redemption to its missiological other—the victims of the global capitalism. The marginalized in the Third World are located at the redemptive site so that the transcendent act of God can reach out to the othered space and redeem it. The contemporary context of empire demands a radical political theology of (economy of) life which de-sovereigns God and re-envisions church as a political ontology of the marginalized. In order to envision God as the de-sovereigned divine and church as the de-imperialized organization, Hardt and Negri propose the theory of *multitude* as a radical, anti-imperial, political subjectivity that resists empire from within.

Multitude is the living alternative that grows within the empire. In Negri's perspective, there are two types of globalization: (1) The empire spreads globally its network of hierarchies and divisions that maintain order through new mechanisms of control and constant conflict; (2) new circuits of cooperation and collaboration that stretch across nations and continents and allow an unlimited number of encounters (Antonio N. & Michael H., 2004: xiii). This is the possibility to live in common in the context of globalization and act together while we remain different. In that sense, *multitude* is the 'negative globalization.' For Negri, *multitude* is an open net work—life in common. Common is not homogeneity but alterity and difference. Unlike the concept of 'people' which is unitary and identitarian, *multitude* is many (Negri & Hardt, 2004: xvii). Multitude is composed of many 'irreducible singularities' of cultures, races, ethnicities, genders, and sexual orientations. *Multitude* is the composed potentiality of all the diverse agents of social production. Unlike the present notion of democracy, in the democracy of *multitude*, the economic, cultural, and the social realms are enacted together to envisage an alternative life in common. It is not just a collection of 'voices of dissent'; rather it is a counter political ontology where all are invited live in a de-imperialized subjectivity. In short, *multitude* is the possibility to envisage a political democracy of 'common' in the age of the empire as we see today in the multiple forms of local struggles for basic necessities of life, food, water, land, and human rights, etc.—the 'commonwealth' of humanity.

Negri's notion of *Commonwealth* articulates the anti-imperial social relations and institutional forms of a possible global democracy. It is a democracy that invites all to share and participate in the common, that is, the air, the water, the fruits of the soil, all nature's bounty—the inhabitance of humanity. Hardt and Negri explain this radical sense of political subjectivity:

> The notion of the common does not position humanity separate from nature, as either its exploiter or its custodian, but focuses rather on the practices of interaction, care, and cohabitation in a common world, promoting the beneficial and limiting the detrimental forms of the common. In the era of globalization, issues of maintence, production and distribution of the common in both senses and in both ecological and socio-economic frameworks became increasingly central (Negri & Hardt, 2009: viii).

With *Commonwealth*, Negri and Hardt conclude the *trilogy* begun with *Empire* and continued in *Multitude*, proposing an ethics of freedom for living in our common world and articulating a possible constitution for radical democracy in the context of empire. It is an invitation to search for a political subjectivity which is ontologically connected to the politics of the *multitude*. To fight against the empire is to search for a life in common—the inhabitance of humanity, the *commonwealth*. What constitutes this ontology of *multitude* or *commonwealth* is our politics of common inheritance—an enmattered subjectivity.

Doesn't this notion of *commonwealth* signify a radical ecclesiology and ecumenism in the contemporary context of the empire?

Ecumenism Re-defined in the Context of Empire

Negri's commonwealth offers the global church or the movement of Ecumenism a radical ontology—the ontology of the *multitude*. According to this ontology, the marginality is not a diaconal space for the church to extend its missiological obligations; rather it is the 'kenotic space' for the church to 'de-activate' its inherent imperial structure. Giorgio Agamben, while defining church as the 'coming community' criticizes that today the Church has become the empire (*oikeo* which means 'dwells like an Empire') and forgets its calling to be a 'coming community'—sojourner (*paroikien*) in this world (Giorgio A., 2012: 2). For him, the Church is not an enclosed community that is constituted for itself or for its 'missiological others.' When we declare that the Church stands for the marginalized, it automatically defines the marginality as the 'exterior other.' Unlike the patristic notion of *oikonomia* (economy of life), marginality is not a 'missiological other' for the church. **Church does not substantiate the marginality within or without; rather the margin is the Church.** Church is a marginal community that resists the imperial logic always. As the crucified body of Christ, the Church nullifies all kinds of imperial logics of discrimination within and envisions a global community of the de-imperialized subjectivities/tortured bodies. Thus, Ecumenism as living in common invokes the Church to be the Church of the crucified people—the marginalized, the agonized, the tortured, the refugees and the enslaved.

Secondly, Ecumenism as living in common denies the imperial logic of 'Oneness' and signifies a democracy of 'multiplicity' which is contrary to the unitary, absolute, totalitarian democracy. *Commonwealth* offers 'a life in common'—a shared solitude—a radical univocity—a radical embodiment—a radical enfleshment. It is not just unity in diversity or commonality between units. *Commonwealth* offers a common realm of being and becoming; but it is always fluid, relational, differential, and materialistic in content. God, according to this logic of multiplicity is also to be located in relationality. Jean-Luc Nancy, in his recent work *Deconstructing Christianity* speaks about God as a *Singular plural*, an ever flowing excess, not just as One (Nancy, 2000). For Alain Badiou, God is an event, out of which we have many meanings and experiences of becoming (Badiou, 2007). Catherine Malabou alludes to the *plasticity* of God. According to Malabou, *plasticity* denies the Western logic of 'One' and offers an existence of 'divine manyness' that substantiates new possibilities for configuring human subjectivity in relationality (Malabou, 209). As Catherine Keller affirms it is an *enmattered God* who 'became flesh'—the inter-carnating God. The challenge before us is to repudiate a sovereign God and envision a crucified God which makes theology anti-imperial.

Thirdly, Ecumenism as living in common offers a radical political ontology which is ecological or materialistic in content. It is a radical enfleshment where all are invited to live in a state of inter-carnality. It is to affirm our *enmattered* subjectivity. Affirming and protecting the elements of Life—water, air, soil, vegetation etc., is nothing but realizing the politics of *commonwealth.* According to this vision, the indigenous people, aboriginals, Dalits, women, the farmers who resist the empire locally and protect the inhabitance of humanity constitute the real *oikos* of God. The human subjectivity is defined here in terms of an *enmattered self. Commonwealth* or living in common is an invitation to search for a political subjectivity which is ontologically connected to the politics of the *multitude.* It is our resistance, to protect the commonwealth and the dignified life of the excluded and the marginalized that provide us the 'ground' for our common social ontology against empire. Michael Marder calls it "vegetal democracy." For Marder, "vegetal democracy is the growing with (and the growing-up) of democracy that hinges on fostering the capacity to live with the countless voices, and especially with the dispersed multiplicity of non-voices and non-identities, that target us both from within and from without: to fall apart in growing-with" (Marder, 2013: 218). The challenge before the present church and Ecumenical Movement is to envision a theology of the *enmattered life*; rather than the economy of life (*oikonomia)*. The theology of *oikoumene* that retains the imperial logic of the church and renders 'marginality' as its 'missiological other' is to be rejected while ecumenism as a radical ontology of the *multitude* and *commonwealth* is to be re-claimed in the contemporary context of empire.

References

Alain Badiou, *Being and Event (*New York: Continuum, 2007).

Antonio Negri & Michael Hardt, *Empire* (Cambridge, M.A: Harvard University Press, 2004).

Antonio Negri. & Michael Hardt, *Multitude: War and Democracy in the Age of Empire*. (New York: Penguin Press, 2004).

Antonio Negri & Michael Hardt, *Commonwealth* (Cambridge, M.A: Harvard University Press, 2012).

Barbara Rossing, "Re-Claiming Oikoumene? Ecumenism, Ecology, and Empire," in *Churasco: A Theological Feast in Honor of Vitor Westhelle*, eds. Mary Philip, John Arthur Nunes and Charles M. Collier (Eugene, Oregon: Pickwick Publications, 2013).

Claude Nicolet, *Space, Geography and Politics in the ealy Roman Empire* (Ann Arbor: University of Michigan Press, 1991).

Catherine Malabou, *Plasticity at the Dusk of Writing: Dialectic, Destruction, Deconstruction, (*New York: Columbia University, 2009).

Giorgio Agamben, *The Kingdom and Glory: For a Theological Genealogy of Economy and Government (*Stanford: Stanford University Press, 2011).

Giorgio Agamben, *The Church and the Kingdom (*London, New York, Calcutta: Seagull Books, 2012).

Jean Luc Nancy,. *Being Singular Plural*. (Stanford: Stanford University Press, 2000).

K.C. Abraham, ed.. 1993. *New Horizons in Ecumenism: Essays in honor of Bishop Samuel Amirtham*. Bangalore: BTESSC & BTTBPSA.

Kessler, D., ed., *Together on the Way: The Harare Report* (Geneva: World Council of Churches, 1998).

Michael Marder, "Vegetal Democracy: The Plant that is not One" in *Politics of the One:*

Concepts of the One and Many in Contemporary Thought, edited by Artemy Magun. (New York: Bloomsbury, 2013).

3

Eschaton, Empire, and the Church*

Introduction

A deliberation on the vocation of Church in the wake of the 500th anniversary of the great Reformation offers both joy and lamentation. The joy is that the Spirit of Reformation as the counter force is still reverberating in the life of the Church as it was presumed by the great reformers 500 years ago. The lamentation is that the Church today still upholds the imperial structures just as it was interrogated by the reformers in the period of Roman papacy. Referring to St. Paul's second letter to Thessalonians (2 Thess. 2: 6-8) Martin Luther argues that the "Pope is the real Antichrist, who has exalted himself above and opposed himself against Christ because he will not permit Christians to be saved without his power" (Luther, 2013: 287). Luther identifies Roman papacy as the restraining force/delaying factor

---

* This essay is the abstract of the presentation held at the National Colloquium organized by SATHRI on the theme *Envisaging Messianic Time: The Agenda for the Transforming Church,* on 8-11th August, 2017 at Tamil Nadu Theological Seminary, Madurai.

(*katechon)* as was the Roman Empire in the first century. According to the reformers, whenever the Church loses its messianic vocation, it becomes another worldly institution—the empire. Reformation demands the Church to fulfill its messianic vocation 'here and now' by de-imperializing its ontology and theology. How does the Church do this de-imperialization within and outside? Will the signs of the time help the Church to recuperate its messianic vocation in the contemporary context of the empire? Then, what would be the anti-imperial eschatology that reconfigures ecclesiology, soteriology, and missiology of the Church today?

Messianic Time/Event/Politics: Listening to St. Paul

The contemporary political philosophers such as Giorgio Agamben, Alain Badiou, Slavoj Zizek, Gilles Deleuze, Michael Hardt, and Antonio Negri find St. Paul as the forerunner of the anti-imperial philosophy and theology. Among them, the Italian philosopher and theologian Giorgio Agamben invites our attention to two Greek words that designate the Church in Pauline writings: *paroikein* and *katoikein. Paroikein* means 'sojourner' and *katoikein* means 'dwell like an empire' (Agamben, 2012: 3). The word 'sojourner' (1 Peter 1.17) designates how a Christian is to live in this world. According to St. Paul, the Church as *ho chronos te paroikas* (Church lives as if in the time of the exile) is to be recalled in its life and ministry. The Church is always called to be in the time of sojourn or exile. This time is not a fixed time according to the chronological order; rather, it is a time that evokes our sense of vocation. Whenever Church loses this time consciousness, its vocation is revoked and becomes a worldly institution–the empire (*katoikein*). For St. Paul, it is the messianic experience of time that signifies the vocation of the Church. St. Paul consciously tries to preserve this 'time-image' (sojourning time) at the heart of his ecclesiology so as to deny the possibility of the Church to 'dwell like an empire' in this world.

The Church assumed its institutional structure during the period of Roman empire. It was the problem of 'the delay of *parousia*' that reoriented the early Christian community to stabilize the institutional and juridical organization of the early Church. Moreover, the Roman Empire claimed its status as the eschatological state. In this particular context, St. Paul had to deny the problem of the 'delay of *parousia*' and to defend the significance of Church as a counter community of kingdom over against the Roman Empire. For Paul, the time between resurrection and *parousia* is not a delayed time as the delay of the train; rather it is the time of the messiah. The time of the messiah never delays. The messianic time is the potential time that comes (*erchetai*) always. Paul reminds the Thessalonians about this notion of ever coming time:

> About dates and times, my friends, we need not write to you, for you know perfectly well that the Day of the Lord comes (*erchetai*) like a thief in the night (1 Thess 5.1-2).

The messiah is called in the gospels *ho erchomenos,* which means 'one who comes', explains the ever-coming nature of the messiah who never ceases to come. Thus, for St. Paul, the messianic time as the qualitative time that remains 'in-between' Jesus' resurrection and second coming signifies the time to experience the messianic vocation of the Church and to witness the crucified/resurrected Christ—the Christ event. The Messianic time is the qualitative time for the Church to reconfigure or re-form itself as the witness (*marturia*) of the Christ-event over against the empire within and out. The Messianic vocation is to re-constitute the Church in its being, becoming, and belonging over against the imperial imaginations. This vocational consciousness of the Church cannot be pushed to the end of history; rather, it is to be fulfilled 'here and now' by confronting the empire in whatever form it remains.

Unlike the traditional understanding of eschatology, Pauline eschatology is not one of apocalypse but one of immediacy. The Greek words, *telos* and *eschaton* denote the end time as the futuristic event. For St. Paul, on the contrary, it is the "paradigm for the understanding of the present time" (Agamben, 2012: 8). It is to envisage *kairos* in *chronos*. It is to experience the end time 'here and now.' One is invited to be drawn by the eschaton 'now.' Unlike the 'realized eschatology,' eschaton is never a delayed reality; rather, it is a present reality. Living today as if living in the end time makes life eschatological. Eternity is no more a futuristic experience; rather, it is present experience of the fullness of time—the time that remains. According to St. Paul, the messianic time is not the end of time but the time of the end. Living in this end time today signifies the messianic vocation of the Church. Agamben elucidates this Pauline emphasis:

> What is messianic is not the end of time but the relation of every moment, every *Kairos*, to the end of time and to eternity. Consequently, what interests Paul is not the final day, the moment at which time ends, but the time that contracts and begins to end. Or one might say, the time that remains between time and its end. (Agamben, 2012: 8).

Pauline literature explains the immediacy of messianic time as it impulses St. Paul to do his ministry of witnessing to the Christ-event even in the context of the forces of torture, alienation and death. Experiencing this time implies a radical reformation in the life of the Church. The consciousness of the messianic time impulses the Church to reclaim the sense of its messianic vocation (*klesis*) here and now. The messianic vocation of the church, first of all, is to uphold a messianic identity. Hardt and Negri, in their political exposition of the anti-imperial ideology—the *Multitude*-argue that St. Paul is convinced about the urgency of envisaging a counter-community of resistance that challenges the overarching nature of the Roman Empire "at the same level of totality" (Hardt & Negri, 2000: 21). Beyond the Jewish nationalistic dreams of political freedom, St. Paul was convinced about the need of a universal 'community of resistance' to counter the overarching logic of the Roman Empire within. St. Paul envisages a community of the messianic event—an event that is of universal significance, a principle that included every person of every nation and that must be spread throughout the entire empire. Agamben explains this:

> The Messianic vocation separates every klesis from itself, engendering a tension with itself, without ever providing it with some other identity; hence, Jew as non-Jew, Greek as non-Greek. (Agamben, 2005: 53).

Messianic vocation invokes the Church to re-constitute the identity on the basis of the crucified identity of Jesus Christ. St. Paul calls this process *katargein,* which means 'inoperativity' or 'de-energizing' or 'de-activating' our juridical subjectivities constituted on the basis of the sovereign law of the imperial state, viz: Jew, Greek, master, slave, man, woman, etc. The identity of the Church is envisaged here as the 'messianic identity' (identity without identity) as it is ontologically connected to the agonistic politics of the tortured people in the world. For St. Paul, the messianic vocation of the Church is to identify itself with the crucified Christ, whose cross summons the weak and the lowborn to sanctification and redemption, and thereby (re-)forms the Church as a community of resistance. Paul explains this messianic identity of the Church:

> But, we have this treasure in earthen vessels, so that it may be clear that this extraordinary power belongs to God and does not come from us. We are afflicted in every way, but not crushed; perplexed, but not driven to despair; persecuted, but not forsaken; struck down, but not destroyed; always carrying about in our body the mortification (*nekrosis*) of Jesus, in order that the life of Jesus may be manifest in our body. For constantly we the living are being handed over into death on account of Jesus, so that the life of Jesus may be manifest in our mortal flesh. (2 Cor. 4:7-11).

According to St. Paul, the Church is called to embody the messianic politics. Cross is the fulcrum of this messianic politics that re-forms the Church as the cruciform body of the agonized. This messianic politics occurs in the consciousness of the messianic time—here and now. Every effort to neglect this cruciform vocation makes the Church a worldly organization—the empire (*katoikein).* The messianic time is the time here and now that invokes, advokes, and provokes the Church to reform itself as a messianic community as it was envisaged by the great reformers 500 years ago. For St. Paul, the Church is the counter-community of those who have no community at all—'the nothings and nobodies of the country"—the uneducated, poor, and low born (1 Cori. 1-26-28). The vocation of the church is to live in this messianic time and its vocation is to become a 'coming community.' Signifying this eschatological ecclesiology, Agamben writes: "living in this time, experiencing this time, is thus not something that the Church can choose, or choose not, to do. It is only in this time that there is a Church at all" (Agamben, 2012: 19). There cannot be a Church without the messianic vocation here and now in confronting the empire within and out. Where do we find such an experience of time and vocation in today's Church?

Reformation as the Messianic Engagement: Listening to the Reformers

For reformers, Reformation is nothing but reclaiming the messianic vocation of the Church over against its desire to become an imperial organization. Reformation as the 'messianic engagement' in the life of the Church disavows the imperial content of its being, becoming and belonging in the world. Denying the sole authority of the papacy, Magisterium, and other imperial patterns that reinstate the priestly power over the common people, reformers instead envisaged an open church, open scripture, and open liturgy in favour of the common believers. It was an effort to dis-close/unveil (*apocalypto*) the institutional structure of the Church and to re-configure it as the peoples' movement. It was a protest (out of which the word 'Protestant' comes from) against the Popes and Cardinals who often lived as empires. They claimed political as well as spiritual power over the people. The Reformation was a prophetic engagement in the life of the Church to retain its messianic vocation—to become a movement of the people of God (Laos) over against its tendency to become a juridical institution—empire in this world.

In reformers' theology of ecclesia, they emphasized the urgency to reclaim it as a protest movement of the laity to challenge the clericalism and the doctrinal supremacy of the institutionalized Church. Concentration of the laity was to delete the binary distinction between the "two estates"—the Church and the state, ecclesia and politics, and to retain the 'irreducible singularity' of the secular. Contrary to medieval Christendom, which hijacked the political/secular realm and ruled over it based on the spiritual power, the Reformation envisaged a more open ecclesiology as it strongly criticized the papal dictatorship and the autocracy of Christendom. As the messianic politics, it was an effort to de-sovereignize the Church and its theology in favour of the common people. It was well-evident in the effort to formulate an open soteriology by critiquing the privatization/marketization of salvation ("Salvation on Sale!") in the Church. Locating in the theology of 'open grace,' the Reformation attuned its performance in an anti-legalistic cartography. As Theodore W. Jennings opines, it was an effort to locate its morality in the 'outlaw justice,'—the justice beyond the Law, which is messianic in content. It is well-evident that the Reformation, as a messianic engagement, envisioned a radical ecclesiology of the *Multitude*—the messianic community of the Christ-event.

Luther affirms the messianic ecclesiology when he shifts it from its status as the communion of saints to the communion of the weak. Luther writes: "The living saints are your neighbors, the naked, the hungry, the thirsty, the poor people who have wives and children and suffer shame" (Althaus, 1996: 50). The sacrament of communion, for Luther, is to partake of the messianic event to identify with the misfortune. Luther writes: "Your heart must go out in love and learn that this is a sacrament of love" (McGrath, 2001: 521). Luther wanted to redeem the sacraments from the 'Babylonian Captivity of the Church' and to offer them the messianic content and practice. The forgiveness that is passed on to the communicants in the messianic event–the eucharist, for Luther, is nothing but the 'ultimate justice'—the justice that goes beyond the captivity of the logic of the institutionalized church. Luther defines the eucharist as the messianic moment of promise and forgiveness through which the community of Christ-event is formulated (McGrath, 2001: 521). The purpose of the formation of this community is to witness the crucified/resurrected Christ over against all kinds of imperial imaginations of domination and exclusion in this world.

By identifying the imperial imaginations of the medieval Church as the delaying factor—*katechon* of the coming of the messiah, the reformers were trying to un-veil/dis-close the enclosed doctrinal imaginations of the imperial Church. Disclosing the enclosed truths signifies a radical apocalyptic moment in the story of Reformation. This apocalyptic/messianic engagement is anti-imperial in content and practice. Its anti-imperial nature is expressed in its political inclination to the agency of the people of God (Laos) in their counter-imagination of Church, sacrament, and theology. The Church in its eucharistic embodiment, is ontologically connected with the weak and the marginalized. The Church in its eucharistic ontology becomes anti-imperial always. As the reformers allude, it is in the encounter with the logic of empire, the Church becomes a messianic community. In Eucharist, as the messianic event, the Church always embodes this anarchical content within, and that spirit keeps it open and inclusive always. When Church becomes an enclosed entity in terms of its doctrines and sacraments, every act of disclosure is eschatological. Thus, *eschaton* is not something that comes from beyond (transcendent); rather it is "in the world as it is, thus", as Agamben writes.

Alluding to the Lutheran reading of Paul, Agamben redefines redemption. Redemption, for Agamben, is not a future oriented hope; rather it is a worldly/temporary event. While explaining his understanding of redemption, Renee D.N van Riessen writes: "Redemption is no longer a question of longing for a different, more perfect and thus redeemed world, nor is it the possibility of relating this world in its state of non-redemption to the coming of a redeeming person or event" (Riessen, 2015). On the other hand, for Agamben, redemption refers to the possibility of seeing the world in the perspective of its "being thus" and of its unfulfilled promises. It is to look at the unfulfilled promises of the present. Agamben's God is not a futurist God, but an immanent God. He says, "Profane is my God.' "Agamben, while speaking about the Church as a messianic community, is hopeful about its potentiality to encounter the enclosed structures of the empire within and out. For Agamben, it is the site of marginality, the state of exception, the bare life that challenges and reforms the Church to be a messianic community. Living in this Eucharistic space, being and becoming this messianic event is the challenge before the Church today.

Reading the Signs of the Times: Recuperating the Messianic Vocation of the Church

For the Church to live in this time of messiah means to read 'the signs of the times' as Mathew calls (Mt. 16:3). Reading 'the signs of times' is to re-form the Church and not to de-form it to 'dwell like an empire.' For the Church, responding to social realities and taking the side of the 'nothings and the nobodies' of this world is to retain its status as a messianic movement—the community of resistance in the contemporary context of the empire. Mordecai's caution to Esther (Esther 4:1-4) is also to discern the signs of the time and to enact her messianic vocation in the particular historical time of empire. Mordecai reminds Esther that her vocation in 'such a time' is to ensure justice to the alienated/tortured people. Esther is reminded of the urgency of the time and to fulfill her vocation by acting upon it immediately. Christian vocation is to be fulfilled by discerning the urgency of the time or 'the need of the hour' as Jesus alludes in the New Testament. For Jesus, 'the hour' (Jn. 2:4) is the hour of his crucifixion, taking the position of a tortured slave in the Roman imperial context.

Christian vocation is always eschatological (messianic) and anti-imperial in content. The biblical tradition of apocalypse is a counter imperial experience as is vividly explained in the book of Revelation. In the traditional interpretation, it is the coming of the day of rapture or doom. The fundamental expressions like Zionism and the American "war on terror" misinterpret the apocalyptical tradition in favor the logic of the empire. Neo-capitalism assumes this eschatology to propagate its consumeristic-market logic of temporality of life by denying the eternal content of human life here and now. Hindu fundamentalists in India are in the mood of ecstasy as they try to re-live the horrors of the Fascist agenda of the Nazi government in Germany in terms of its politics of annihilation of the minorities and the marginalized. However, the book of Revelation dis-closes (apocalypse) the end of the empire and the beginning of a new community of resistance founded around the power of the slain Lamb (Rev. 21: 1-5). The Greek word *hypomene* (Rev. 1:9) which is used in the book of Revelation frequently signifies the 'patient endurance' or the 'resistance' of the tortured community. Barbara Rossing, the American biblical scholar explains this very well:

> By their patient and subversive life style of love and welcome and community, the early Christians resisted the claims of the empire. They lived in light of the vision of the Lamb that had changed their lives. And people around them marveled at their joy and boldness (Rossing, 2004: 17).

In the contemporary world of sovereign powers and the systems of exclusion how does the Church recuperate its messianic vocation? How does the Church become the community of the agonized when the Church itself become the empire? If Reformation stems out of the Church's messianic vocation to become an anti-imperial movement of the agonized people here and now, do we need to wait for one or many more Reformations in the life of the Church in the days to come? As Mordecai reminds Esther, it is also high time for the Church to recall its *klesis* and thereby reform its ecclesiology, Christology, missiology and eschatology in favour of the crucified in this world.

Or will some of these signs of the time help the Church finally grasp the historical occasion and recover its messianic vocation here and now?

> *My father was begging them to stop. He kept saying we had gone to pick up a dead cow, but they insisted we had killed it. They made us take of four shirts, tied us to a vehicle and used big lathis to hit us. More than 50 people were watching us get beaten, including some policemen, but no one helped. Instead, they were filming it on mobile phones. We would never kill an animal. When it is dead they call us to remove the carcass. For centuries, our community has done this work. Why are they suddenly talking about cow protection?* (*Frontline*, August 19, 2016, 117-121).
>
> (Vasram Sarvaiya, 23 years old, one of the four Dalits who were beaten up on July 11, 2016 by gau rakshaks (cow protectors) in Gujarat).

> *There is a new climate of fear in India about speaking freely on some subjects. If they make their points, or even if they invite someone to present a point of view, they may be in danger of losing their job (The Economic Times,* February 26, 2017).
>
> (Amartya Sen's response on the suspension of Rajasree Ranawat, Professor of English at Jai Narain Vyas University, Jodhpur, for inviting professor Nivedita Menon of Jawaharlal Nehru University, New Delhi. February 26, 2017).
>
> *Maas khate hai, maaro inko* (they eat meat, kill them) (*Frontline*, July 21, 2017).
>
> (The Hindu fundamentalists who brutally murdered Junaid Khan, 16-year-old Muslim boy on a train from Delhi bound for Mathura on June 26, 2017).

Post-script

The task of the (reforming) Church is to retain its messianic vocation here and now. The reading the signs of the times is to reconstitute itself as the messianic community of the slain Lamb. Messianic community is an open community—re-formed community—that never allows it to become a kyriarchal, patriarchal, juridical organization—the empire. As a community of resistance, the Church never compromises with the structures of domination and exclusion. Resistance (*hypomene*) is its joyful vocation to be fulfilled here and now. To lose this vocation is to lose its existence today. The lynched Dalits, the uprooted Adivasis, the raped women, the farmers at the brink of suicide, the jobless traditional workers, the minorities who live in the threat of genocide etc. are no more the diaconal stations of the Church to be reached out; rather, they are the *eschata*—the end time here and now. It is the site of new beginning—the epiphany of the new heaven and new earth, and of course the new Church. It is this vision of apocalypse we are drawn to by faith and love. Dragged to such a radical apocalypse is something passionate, obsessive and revolutionary as the Song of Solomon speaks about love/sex;

> Let me be kissed with your mouth's kiss for your loves are better than wine, fragrant with your best anointments. Your name is oil poured out; and so the young girls have taken delight in you. Drag me after you—let us run! May the king lead me into his storerooms so that we might exult and rejoice in you. Mindful of your lives above wine they rightly delight in you.

(Song of Solomon 1: 2-4; translated from the Latin of the New Vulgate by Paul J. Griffiths).

Let us run into this love, passion, and apocalypse and become heirs of eternity here and now.

References

Alister E. McGrath, *Christian Theology: An Introduction,* (UK: Blackwell Publishing, 1991).

Barbara Rossing, *The Rupture Exposed: The Message of Hope in the Book of Revelation,* (USA: Westview Press, 2004).

Giorgio Agamben. 2005. *The Time That Remains: A commentary on the Letter to the Romans*, trans. Patricia Dailey (Sanford: Calif.: Stanford University Press, 2005).

Giorgio Agamben, *The Church and the Kingdom*, trans. Leland de Durantaye, (London, New York, Calcutta: Seagull Books, 2012).

Martin Luther, *Luther's Work* (Philadelphia: Fortress Press, 1995-1986).

Martin Luther, *Schmalkaldische Artikel*, 2.4. Cited in Ward Blanton and Hent de Vries, ed., *Paul and the Philosophers*, ed. (USA: Fordham University Press, 2003).

Michael Hardt & Antonio Negri, *Empire* (Cambridge, Massachusetts: Harvard University Press, 2000).

Paul Althaus, *The Theology of Martin Luther* (Philadelphia: Fortress press, 1996).

Renee D.N. Riessen, "Community and its Other, Remarks on Giorgio Agamben's *The Coming Community* from Levinasian point of view," *Zeitschrift fur Diolektische Theologie*, Supplement Series 5, 2015.

4

Religion, Power and Empire: Ambedkar as Guide*

Introduction

Religion as a modern Western concept has always been embodied with its "imperio-colonial sense"—the ethos of transcendence (Mark Lewis Taylor, 2011: 17). As Gayatri Chakravorty Spivak, the postcolonial feminist thinker argues, religion as it is "deeply implicated in the narrative of the ebb and flow of power" is impotent to resist the logic of the empire unless it is decolonized in content and practice (Spivak 1999: 382). By naming the empire as the context of contemporary Christian mission and exposing the imperio-colonial sense of world religions, CWM in fact invokes us to formulate a two-fold radical vision of mission: firstly, to envisage an anti-imperial global community that particularly stands in solidarity with the

* Paper presented at the International Conference on Empire and Mission, organized by Council of World Mission (CWM), Bangkok, Thailand on 28 May-2 June 2017.

marginalized and excluded; secondly, to re-define religion as an ethico-political practice of justice by repudiating its imperio-colonial sense embodied in dogmatics and doctrines.

Marks C. Taylor, the political theologian from North America has clearly exposed the return of Christianity in the post-modern period in connection with the emergence of global capitalism (Taylor, 2004: 30). According to Taylor, global capitalism and its neoliberal social imaginations are legitimized by Christian theology in the postmodern period. It is rightly said in the DARE concept note "In many postmodern contexts, (Christian) God becomes oppressive, narcissistic and anti-human" (2017: 5). The global capitalist agenda has become a decisive economic/cultural/political propaganda in the contemporary world community and it has assumed the form of the empire that enjoys the patronage of Christian Theology. The election victory of Donald Trump as the new President of the United States of America testifies to this fact and it has become a crucial vantage point for the pro-capitalist and neoliberal Christian theologians to chant their liberal liturgies and theologies. However, the illegitimate relationship between the empire and the Church is not just a modern or postmodern phenomenon; rather, it can be traced back even in the history of the church to the Constantine/Patristic Era. Whether it is the hierarchical pattern of society or the question of the social exclusion of the weaker sections, the Western logic of empire always finds its legitimacy in Christian dogmatics based on the notion of the sovereign God and His charity-oriented love for the other. Giorgio Agamben exposes the imperial meaning of the patristic theology of *oikoumene* (economy of salvation) as it legitimizes the absolute difference between God and the world while assuming a fake unity of divine love. Mission in this theology has been interpreted as a benevolent act of the wholly other God who wants to redeem 'the other' without compromising His absolute otherness. Mission without challenging the notion of the benevolent act of the sovereign God becomes a charity-oriented program of the 'civilized to the uncivilized', which is foundational to the modern Christian mission.

Mission in the context of the empire, however, has to relocate its theological foundation in a de-colonized Christianity and a de-transcendentalized divinity. Mission in the postcolonial context demands the repudiation of the "imperio-colonial sense" of Christianity and its metaphysical dogmatics that legitimizes the notion of God from "beyond" (transcendence). It is this notion of 'beyond' God that justifies the colonial act of mission. In his well-read book *Deconstructing Christianity*, Jean-Luc Nancy (2008: 87) demands the crucifixion of the Christian logic of the sovereign power implicated in the monotheist theology of God and the decolonization of the Euro-centric content of Christian dogmatics and doctrines. Gianni Vattimo, on the other hand, argues for a "weak ontology" or "the ontology of the weakening of (the Western) Being", which supplies philosophical reasons for preferring a non-totalitarian divinity and social democracy. According to Vattimo, Western Christian theology and democracy have to be re-constituted on the basis of this "weak ontology" in order to envisage a liberal, tolerant, and democratic society that attends to the cry of the victims of this world (Vattimo, 2003: 91-92). In the same vein of thought, Spivak offers a postcolonial notion of "de-transcendentalized transcendence"—a notion of divinity that is re-located in the immediate, the material, and the local (Moore and Rivera, 2011: 71).

While defining the empire, Michael Hardt and Antonio Negri (2000) argue that it is no more a military system of oppression or just an economic propaganda; rather it is a new form of ontology of sovereignty. For them, the empire is a new form of sovereign power that forms the subjectivities in favour of its neo-capitalist agendas and hierarchical ordering of global communities. They expose its multidimensional operations of anarchy and hierarchy in favour of the multinational corporations and the global elite. For Hardt and Negri, the empire is no more a military system that exercises its repressive power over its subjects; rather it is a biopower that colonizes the minds and bodies of its subjects and enables them to be the agents of the sovereign systems. The empire today appears in the forms of economic, cultural, and political agendas that constitute the structure of the global community. Negri, thus calls the empire a new form of sovereignty that reconstitutes global community in terms of asymmetric social relationships. They call it a sovereign power because there is no outside of this enclosed ontology. Even the resistance can be the legitimization of the logic of Empire. Hardt argues that even the acts of terrorism are not to resist the empire but to control the empire. Even in this crucial juncture of human entrapment, however, Hardt and Negri find fecundity in religion, especially in the theological imagination of *ekklesia* to become the counter imperial social imagination to reclaim the 'life in common' over against the homogenous logic of the empire. However, they are convinced of the need to the de-colonization of Christianity and its dogmas and doctrines as they substantiate the hierarchical ordering of social sections.

In this process of our effort to de-imperialize Christian vision and mission, this paper tries to contribute its part by bringing the discussion of an indigenous effort that re-defines religion as the ethico-political practice of the marginalized, as it critically engages with the imperio-colonial sense of world religions. Apart from Christianity and other world religions, this particular indigenous philosophy of religion finds fecundity in the materialist philosophies and ideologies in order to substantiate an anti-imperial social order and social existence in favour of the marginalized. It is the story of the Indian Dalit legend, Babasaheb Ambedkar, who has offered a political philosophy of religion through which he disavowed the Brahmanic imperial ethical practices of caste which have been legitimized by orthodox Hinduism. Ambedkar is the first Indian philosopher who critically engages with world religions such as Hinduism, Buddhism, Islam, and Christianity, and exposed their "imperio-colonial sense" in favour of the marginalized communities in India—the Dalits. Ambedkar renounced the concept of religion and at the same time formulated a radical philosophy of Dhamma—the political becoming of the social. This essay particularly focuses on Ambedkar's re-definition of religion as Dhamma as it repudiates the imperial notion of divine sovereign power and colonial dogmatism of the world religions, including Christianity. This study envisages a radical re-definition of religion as an ethico-political practice of justice in which the dichotomy between religion and politics, philosophy and ethics, secular and sacred, East and West, and the West and the Rest, is denied. This essay envisions that this discussion will invoke us to re-draft our Christian mission in a postcolonial world, where the marginalized sections of our global community expose the illegitimate nexus between Christianity and empire; theology and politics.

Ambedkar: Religion as the Moral Conscience

Ambedkar, as the political thinker of the subalterns in India in the period of colonial modernity, exposes the hegemonic epistemological foundation of the Indian socio-political order, which excludes a majority of the people on account of the social practice—caste—that is legitimized by orthodox Hindu epistemology and theology. Ambedkar was convinced about the permanent inconsistency in the political knowledge of Indian casteist social order where the majority of people are permanently excluded and their struggle to enter into the political domain that constitutes democracy in India is inherently problematic. In this contested political situation, Ambedkar comes up with a radical slogan: the social precedes political (Kesava Kumar, 2008: 193). According to Ambedkar, it is the social content of democracy that enhances the excluded one's struggles to reorganize the social-political order. It is not just the lack of political conscience, but the lack of moral conscience that becomes important in the Indian context of caste exclusion. For Ambedkar, the moral conscience is the religious content of social organization that re-orders the society in favour of justice and equality. Thus, Ambedkar critically engages with orthodox Hinduism that substantiates caste practice and seeks for alternative religious foundations in favour of justice and equality.

According to Ambedkar, the Indian social order, which is fundamentally built on the caste epistemology of Vedic religiosity, is to be destabilized and denied on the basis of the modern ideals of democracy, justice, and liberty. The moral standard of Vedic religiosity is not at all acceptable due to its exclusivist and enslaving theology. The authoritarian Hindu social order delimits the freedom and enslaves the majority of the Indian polity. The victims of the caste system are thrown out of the socio-political and economic capitals of the society. They are regarded as the outcastes and the untouchables of the country. Thus, the social order is to be reconstituted on the basis of equality, justice, and moral religiosity.

Hinduism is not capable enough to provide an ethical social life due to its caste epistemology. It is here Ambedkar brings the question of religious conversion as the political strategy for freedom and social democracy. For Ambedkar, renouncing Hinduism, is a political strategy of Dalits to merge with a political community and to have a political identity in the context of colonial modernity.

Ambedkar: Religion as the Political Community of the Marginalized

Religion, for Ambedkar, is nothing but a political community that gives a collective identity to the marginalized people in India. Especially the modern Indian context of nation-state necessitates a collective political identity that is rooted in a religious identity. In the nation-state politics, it is the religious collective identity that signifies the representation of plural sections of people. Analyzing this consciously, Ambedkar argues for a religious identity for the caste victims to be represented in the nation-state political power. Thus, the notion of community becomes central to Ambedkar's political philosophy, which is closely linked with the desire for a radical religious identity. For him, Hinduism is not qualified to be a just community or a fair religion. It is a collection of rules and regulations that substantiate hierarchy of human beings and the super beings. Hinduism, for Ambedkar, is a worthless philosophy of life that never accepts the worth of human beings. For him, Hinduism is a fake religion that still remains in the age old myths that substantiate the hierarchical ordering of the social order. In the same way, he was critical of Islam and Christianity due to their impotency to challenge the caste epistemology and its practices, even though they stand for egalitarianism.

For Ambedkar, Buddhism has the inherent potentiality to be a moral community based on political reasoning and ethics. Buddhism, unlike Islam and Christianity, has had the history of challenging caste epistemology theologically and politically. Ambedkar finds fecundity in the Buddhist philosophy of ethics as he engages with it critically and re-defined it as the Navayana Buddhism. Contrary to the Marxist notion of class, Ambedkar's ideal community is to be created through the moral transformation of an individual from caste status to political subjectivity. Ambedkar believes that reformed Buddhism has the potential to initiate this moral transformation because of its anti-casteist epistemological heritage and the moral philosophy of political becoming through *sangh* (community). In the law's place, he advocated the criterion of a new socio-cultural-political community as the power capable of producing social consciousness and a shared moral order. Conversion to Buddhism was a political agenda of Ambedkar to envisage a political community, a political practice, a counter symbolic space, and a political theology that challenged the casteist social order and promoted political subjectivity to the disenfranchised in the Indian context.

Ambedkar: Religion as the Ethico-Political Practice of Justice

Following the Navayana Buddhist philosophy, Ambedkar defines religion as a political philosophy of Dhamma—the ethico-political practice of Justice. He distinguishes between religion and Dhamma. For him, religion is personal whereas Dhamma is social. According to Ambedkar, Hinduism as a reformed Brahmanic philosophy, is ritualistic and thus forms enslaving subjectivities. On the other hand, Dhamma stands for righteousness, which means right relationship with all. Dhamma necessitates a socio-political relationship and vice versa. Society cannot do without Dhamma. Dhamma leads to liberty and justice. Dhamma consists of *prajna* (reason) and *karuna* (compassion). It is the understanding with compassion and ethics that keeps our social life righteous and democratic (Ambedkar, 2011: 221). Following Buddha, Ambedkar held the view that religion is connected with revealing the beginning of things or the origin of the world whereas Dhamma is to reconstruct the world. Dhamma is founded on morality and thus it is built on immanence while religion is founded on transcendence. For religion, morality is an attachment since it is linked with the notion of a 'beyond' God; whereas as in Dhamma, morality takes the place of God, although there is no God in Dhamma. Morality in Dhamma does not need any divine sanction or legitimization from beyond. It arises out of the human relationship for liberty, freedom and justice that is envisaged in the political philosophy of Dhamma.

Morality in Dhamma is considered as sacred because it stands for the protection of the weak. Survival of the weakest is the social imperative behind the morality. It is the morality or the politics of the survival of the weakest that determines the sacrality of the socio-political life. Sacredness is neither beyond the socio-political life nor does it substantiate any hierarchical social order within. Unlike religion, Dhamma is not controlled by ceremonies, rituals and liturgies, rather by social morality that sustains the society as sacred. For Ambedkar, Dhamma is not just rhetorical, rather it is practical and thus internally political. It is our effort to make our society more ethical and moral that determines the divine content of the social life. God is not regarded as a legitimizing point: rather it is the ultimate ethos of responsibility that invokes us always to strive for a just-moral community. The transformation of the society is not linked with any transcendental logic: rather it is embodied in the political formation of just relationships. It is here Ambedkar's political theology of (no) God finds semblance with the argument of Giorgio Agamben, the post-continental philosopher, when he says "God is not revealed "in" the world, but the world itself, as it is thus, and insofar as it is absolutely and irreparably profane, is God" (2003: 93) . God as the divine potentiality is in the "being thus" of things which is materialist in content. Of course, Catherine Keller's dictum becomes more significant here: "If God is immaterial, God doesn't matter" (2009: 112). Ambedkar's political philosophy of (no) God provokes Christian theology to seek for an embodied, enfleshed, and enmattered God who is the "being thus" of all political practices of justice, freedom, and equality.

Ambedkar: Critiquing Christianity as the Religion of Transcendence

Despite its egalitarianism, Ambedkar is skeptic about the potentiality and the usefulness of Christian theology in challenging the caste knowledge and its practices. According to Ambedkar, Christianity is purely spiritual and transcendental. Christian spirituality is unrelated to the material life and thus it is politically unproductive for the marginalized. Ambedkar argues that it is evident in the life of the Dalits who converted to Christianity. The Christian converted Dalits, in Ambedkar's perspective, become apolitical and inactive due to the transcendent content of the Christian doctrines. Analyzing the missionized theology in India, Ambedkar tries to expose the theological inconsistency within the doctrinal discourses of Christian missionary program:

> Instead of being taught that their fall was due to a wrong social and religious environment and that for their environment they must attack the environment, they were taught their fall was due to their sin. Consequently, the Dalit Christians instead of being empowered to conquer their environmental context, conferred themselves with the belief that there is no use of struggling, for the simple reason that their fall is due to the sin committed not by them but by some remote ancestors of theirs, called Adam and Eve. (Ambedkar 1989: 471-2).

According to James Massey, here Ambedkar stresses that when a Dalit Christian "was a Hindu his fall was due to his *karma*. When he becomes a Christian he learns that his fall is due to the sins of his ancestor. In either case, there is no escape for him" (2003: 60). In Ambedkar's political philosophy, the transcendental framework of Christianity is being strongly interrogated and the Christian theology is being invoked to deconstruct its doctrinal fecundity in a postcolonial political content.

Signifying Ambedkar's Political Philosophy of Religion in the Contemporary Indian Context of Empire

In the contemporary Indian political context, the Hindutva ideology—the political philosophy of orthodox Hinduism with the support of the current political governance of the country—enforces the age-old casteist and hierarchical social patterns for the sake of reinstating pseudo-nationalist heritages. The women, the poor, the Dalits/Adivasis, the tribals, and the unorganized sections of the country face various kinds of violence and violations. The Dalits are being tortured in the name of their menial jobs, food culture and social position, as it is imposed upon them on the basis of caste phenomenology. Hindutva ideology with its political power assumes a new form of the empire in India today. Ambedkar's political philosophy of justice (Dhamma) becomes more significant today as it invokes the formation of the radical political community that stands for the weaker sections. Hindutva as a transcendent ideology legitimizes a sacred 'beyond' in order to substantiate the hierarchical ordering of the society. Dhamma offers a sharp critique of this transcendental legitimacy of the sacred and seeks radical political practices of justice to restructure the social imagination in favour of the weak and vulnerable, especially the Dalits. What is interesting is that the present Hindutva government offers venerations of Ambedkar effigies, while consciously suppressing any kind of eruptions of his ideological manifestations.

The Church in India, which has had the heritage of challenging the sovereign powers of the state, become silent and mute due to its fear on the closure of their institutions such as educational institutions and hospitals, their major income-generating programs. Furthermore, as we have discussed earlier the Church in India is yet to develop a radical political theology of justice as it encounters the new nuances of the empire. For that matter, Ambedkar's political philosophy of justice becomes a meaningful interlocutor to envisage a relevant postcolonial, anti-imperial, materialist, political theology in India today. Christian theology is invoked here to envisage a materialist turn, repudiating the sovereignty of the wholly other God and to take an immanent turn to become the "being thus" of the political practice of justice. Indian Christian theology including Dalit theology never engaged with this materialist notion of (no) God.

Secondly, Ambedkar's political philosophy of religion invites Christian theology to have a postcolonial turn to de-colonize its Euro-centric dogmatics and doctrines. As Catherine Keller contends while delineating the potentiality of postcolonial theologies in the contemporary context of the empire, "With its (Christian Theology's) imperial success, the Church, one might argue, absorbed an idolatry of identity: a metaphysical Babel of unity, an identity that homogenizes the multiplicities it absorbs, that either excludes or subordinates every creaturely other, alter, subaltern" (2004:223). The challenge that the Ambedkar's philosophy of religion poses before Christian theology is that it is to be rooted in the subaltern ethical and religious epistemologies embodied in their political practices of transformation; rather than the Euro-centric "imperio-colonial" epistemologies and doctrines that are impotent in resisting the Vedic-transcendental epistemologies and theologies. The challenge before Christian theology in India is to reconfigure its epistemological and philosophical foundations that delimit its potential to become a subaltern political practice which locates its epistemological habitation in Indian materialistic philosophies and heterodox religious traditions.

Finally, Ambedkar's philosophy of religion invites Christian Theology to take a polydoxical turn. Polydoxy, as Catherine Keller and Laurel C. Schneider define, signifies the multiple origins of its resources such as doxa, opinion, heritage, and tradition. As Edward Said once said, "the origin is always plural." Polydoxy, as it celebrates multiplicity, manyness and pluralism, denies any kind of fundamentalism as we see in the case of Hindutva ideology. Unlike the orthodox tradition, Polydoxy celebrates inter-disciplinarity, trans-disciplinarity and even non-disciplinarity. It is to encounter, articulate, embody and contest the multiplicity of Indian religious traditions in favour of the weak and the agonized. As Richard Kearney opines, Polydoxy is the *anatheist* point where the so-called theists and atheists sit together, dream together, and do theology/politics together for the disenfranchised. For the Church it is an invitation to validate the multiplicity of its being, becoming and belonging in this world of manyness. Religion in this polydoxical turn becomes 'religion without religion' and it is the moment when Christianity is provoked to be a kenotic Christianity (Christianity without religion: Dietrich Bonhoeffer). In other words, the context of empire is the polydoxic moment for the Christian church to deny the fixity of its dogmatics and the idolatry of its traditions and thereby de-imperialize itself.

References

Aakash Singh Rathore and Ajay Verma, eds. *B. R. Ambedkar: the Buddha and his Dhamma, A Critical Edition* (New Delhi: Oxford University Press, 2011).

Anupama Rao, "Revisiting interwar thought: Stigma, labor, and the immanence of caste-class," in *The Political Philosophies of Antonio Gramsci and B. R. Ambedkar: Itineraries of Dalits and Subalterns,* edited by Cosimo Zene (London & New York: Routledge, 2013).

B. R. Ambedkar: *Writings and Speeches,* edited by Vasant Moon and Hari Narke, Vol. 17 (3): 503 (Mumbai Education Department, Government of Maharashtra).

Catherine Keller and Laurel C. Schneider, eds., *Polydoxy, Theology of Multiplicity and Relation* (London and New York: Routledge, 2011).

Gayatri Chakravorty Spivak, *A critique of Postcolonial Reason: Towards a History of the Vanishing Present* (Cambridge, M.A: Harvard University Press, 1999).

Gianni Vattimo, *Nihilism & Emancipation: Ethics, Politics, and Law* (New York: Columbia University Press, 2003), 91-92.

Giorgio Agamben, *The Coming Community,* trans. M. Hardt (Minneapolis: University of Minnesota, 2005).

Harish Wankhede, "'The Political and Social in the Dalit Movement Today,' in *Economic & Political Weekly,* February 9, 2008, 50-57.

James Massey, *Dr. B. R. Ambedkar, A Study in Just Society* (New Delhi: Center for Dalit/Subaltern Studies, 2003).

Jean-Luc Nancy, *Dis-Enclosure: The Deconstruction of Christianity,* trans. Bettina Bergo, Gabreil Malenfant, and Michael B. Smith (New York: Fordham University Press, 2008).

Kancha Illaiah, *God as Political Philosopher: Budhha's Challenge to Brahmanism* (Calcutta: Samya, 2000).

Kesava Kumar, "Political Philosophy of B.R. Ambedkar: A Critical Understanding," in *International Research Journal of Social Sciences,* Vol 1, No. 2, pp 193-210, 2008, Pondicherry University, Pondicherry.

Mark C. Taylor, *Confident Games: Money and Markets in a World Without Redemption* (Chicago: University of Chicago Press, 2004).

Michel Hardt and Antonio Negri, *Empire* (Cambridge, M.A: Harvard University Press, 2009).

Mark Lewis Taylor, *The Theological and The Political: On the Weight of the World* (Minneapolis: Fortress Press, 2011).

Pradeep Gokhale, ed., *The Philosophy of Dr. B. R. Ambedkar* (Pune: Indian Philosophical Quarterly Publication, 2008).

Valerian Roudrigues, ed., *The Essential Writings of B. R. Ambedkar* (New Delhi: Oxford University Press, 2002).

5

Theological Education as Transformative Politics*

Introduction

Let me begin with an experience that I have faced in one of my classes on feminist theology. It was a discussion on the violence against women, specifically on rape victims. Neglecting my passion and sensitivity on the issue, a few students seemed indifferent in the class. I asked them the reason. They said: "Sir, don't you know about the counselling tips for the rape victims? Now healing process of the rape victims has become easier and simple. Then why should we worry about it?" Does our theological education make our budding theologians insensitive, impervious, impassionate, and oblivious? Does our theological education lose its critical edge and become apolitical in content? Or is it because of the over emphasis

---

* Talk offered at the international consultation organized by Council of World Mission & Senate of Serampore and Bishop's College, Kolkata on 28-30 November, 2016

on the 'compassionate' ministry of the established churches not to intervene in the political process of the healing of communities but to remain within the sacramental witness of salvation through their liturgical discourses? If then, what kind of transformation does our theological education have to envision today to make our Church and theological academia politically sensitive?

Mark Lewis Taylor argues that it is the 'ethos of transcendence' that helps Christian theology to be insensitive to the agonistic politics of the tortured bodies in the world, and at the same time to offer a sacramental theology of salvation through its liturgical discourses (Taylor, 2011: xi). The 'rehabilitation' of trans-genders is comfortable for the diaconal and sacramental witness of the Churches in India. On the other hand, the Church in India is silent in the public space with regard to the political issues connected with sex and gender. The 'ethos of transcendence', as it legitimizes a point of salvation outside or beyond the 'weight of the world' or the agonistic politics of the tortured bodies in the world, makes the Church/ theological academia comfortable in keeping this double stand. The transformatory politics, as practiced by the Church, is founded on transcendental ethics, theology, liturgy, and politics, which necessitate reconstruction especially in the emerging context of the biopolitics of the tortured bodies in this world. This is the major methodological challenge that is faced by the theological academia today.

To make contemporary theological education a redemptive politics of transformation, Christian theology has to envisage certain methodological re-imaginations. This paper offers three specific methodological shifts, viz: the turn towards immanence, the turn towards messianic politics, and the turn towards *theopoiesis*, for envisaging a redemptive politics and theology as part of the public witness of the churches and theological communities in India. The first section of this paper tries to expose the 'ethos of transcendence,' as Taylor calls it, which substantiates the transcendental ethics/ politics/theology of transformation by neglecting the political becoming of the tortured bodies from within. Engaging with the Italian philosopher Giorgio Agamben, who offers a theology of radical immanence, this section offers a critique of the political theology of transformation. The second section discusses some methodological re-imaginations to counter the transcendental ethics/theology/politics of transformation and offers three specific theological turns by which the theological program re-locates itself as the *theopoiesis.* Becoming *theopoiesis,* theology envisages a polydoxical—secular—materialist epistemological ground based on its theology of the political ontology of salvation exemplified in the crucified body of Jesus Christ.

Theology, Politics, and Trans-formation: Exorcising the 'Ethos of Transcendence'

While tracing the genealogy of the Western notion of politics, Giorgio Agamben contends that the entire history of the Western political thought bears the horrors of totalitarianism due to its foundation in the notion of sovereign state/God (Agamben, 1998: 11). Agamben argues that in the notion of sovereignty or the totalitarianism of the state, the natural life (*zoe*) is denied at the same time it is presupposed within the political life (*bios*). In the Roman imperial logic, no human being is stateless. When you fail to become a citizen of the (law) state, according to Agamben, you are automatically becoming a no-human— *Homo Sacer* —'a bearer of life to which anything at all can be done'. Agamben calls this state of life as 'bare-life' or 'state of exception' where certain people live outside of the protection of the law of the state (*bios*). The people who live at this 'state of exception,' the slaves, the refugees, the inhabitants of the camps, the immigrants, the unborn, the stateless are excluded from official legal protection and reduced to a state of 'bare-life' where they could be slaughtered, ignored, starved, tortured, and imprisoned for life. This exclusion is legally sanctioned and thus they are in a state of 'excluded in' or the 'included out.' Agamben argues that this state of exception or the legally sanctioned system of exclusion as the biopolitics of sovereignty has never been attended by Western political thinkers and theologians.

Agamben theorizes the biopolitical impact of the sovereignty that forms, reforms, and deforms the public life. In this logic, there is no natural life (*zoe*) outside of the effect of sovereignty. Thus, life, whether it is biological or political, it is nothing but biopolitical—an act of sovereignty. Agamben identifies a permanent fracture between life and politics in the history of Western political thought which cannot be rectified and thus the political theories, theologies, struggles, and manifestoes of the past two and half millennia become insufficient to reckon with this crisis. It is here the so-called political theologies are also interrogated and challenged. Political theologies in the West have never challenged the inherent notion of sovereign state/God as it legitimizes the state of exception—the bare-life–the inherent political system of exclusion. What he tries to communicate is that there is no pure politics to be theorized as a political thought which is detached to the discursive power of the sovereignty. He explains this in *Homo Sacer*:

> Until a completely new politics—that is a politics no longer founded on the exception of bare life—is at hand, every theory and every praxis will remain imprisoned and immobile, and the 'beautiful day' of life will be given citizenship only either through blood and death or in the perfect senselessness to which the society of the spectacle condemns it (Agamben, 1998: 19).

Agamben put himself at odds with other political thinkers and theologians who hold hope in the contemporary democratic engagements and in the development of a culture of human rights. Agamben's sharp criticism of the current political engagement is based on its inadequacy to recognize the problem of the inherent politicization of life—the biopolitics of the sovereign state/God. For Agamben, it is impossible to get rid of this politicization of life or biopolitics of the sovereign power, and any attempt to resist it will ultimately become an entrenchment of the very powers that is mobilized against. It is here Agamben brings his notion of messianic politics in dialogue with his major interlocutor-Walter Benjamin. Messianic politics is not just a politics of trans-formation; rather it is exorcising or the inoperativity of the biopolitics of the sovereign power inscribed on human bodies.

Redemption is not a transcendent experience of transformation; rather it is inherent in the political becoming of the tortured bodies as it is exemplified in the crucified body of Jesus Christ. It is an immanent experience of salvation where "the orgasmic power erected out of the flux of pain and the bio-salvatory energy sprout out of the wounds of the crucified body" offers the radical memory of redemption of the crucified bodies today (Mbembe, 2001: 235). The politics of redemption is inherent in the political becoming of the crucified bodies in the agonistic world today as it is erupted out of the suicide body of Rohit Vemula and the unnumbered tortured bodies in this world. Redemption for Agamben is not a future oriented hope; rather it is an embodied experience in the social bodies or "in the world as it is, thus". As Renee D.N. van Riessen writes, "Redemption is no longer a question of longing for a different, more perfect and thus redeemed world, nor is it the possibility of relating this world in its state of non-redemption to the coming of a redeeming person or event" (Riessen: 2015). In Agamben, redemption refers to the possibility of seeing the world at the same time from the perspective of its 'being thus' and of its unfulfilled promises. Thus, Agamben's political thought recommends concentrating on the present and its unfulfilled promises of redemption. The politics of redemption emerges out of the bio-politics of the tortured bodies which is founded on the act of exorcising the 'ethos of transcendence,' and located in a political ontology of salvation as it is signified in the crucified body of Jesus Christ.

Towards the Politics of Redemption: Methodological Re-imaginations

Theological education in India as the pedagogy of transformation has enriched the Church/theological academia to encounter with the bio-politics of the empire. However, its foundation is in the logic of sovereignty of God and thereby becomes unable to attend the inherent politicization of life in the world of empire, making Christian theology insignificant to attend the redemptive politics of the tortured bodies in this world. On the other hand, Christian theology through its liturgical discourses offers salvation to the crucified bodies from outside or beyond. Theological insensitivity to the political issues of the excluded bodies is not just a functional issue of Christian theology; rather it is a fundamental problem of its foundation in the 'ethos of transcendence', by which it offers salvation from beyond. Unless and until its 'ethos of transcendence' is exorcised, Christian theology can never be a politics of redemption in this world. To make our contemporary theological education a radical politics of redemption, Christian theology has to envisage certain methodological re-imaginations in the context of the emergence of the bio-politics of the crucified bodies against the dispositions of the sovereign power.

First of all, it has to take an **immanent turn.** The turn towards immanence envisages an immanent God—God without the logic of transcendence. God from beyond (transcendence) always legitimizes the 'transcendental ethics and politics', which sanction the logic of redemption from outside (trans-formation). The methodology of radical immanence offers a theology of an enmattered God who is inherently involved in the political process of being, becoming and belonging, and envisages transformation from within. The politics of the divine enfleshment envisages a redemptive biopolitics of the crucified and a theology of plasticity embodied in the political process of becoming and belonging. The enfleshment of God envisages the social ontology of salvation which has been exemplified through the crucified body of Jesus Christ.

The immanent God is a God who cannot be a sovereign-transcendent power. Agamben argues that God is not revealed "in" the world, but the world itself, as it is thus, and insofar as it is absolutely and irreparably profane, is God. God is in the "being thus" of things. Agamben interprets this "being thus" as to be exposed, abandoned and without shelter. Jesus on the cross signifies this God without shelter—the one who became the 'body without organs' in the time of incarnation. In this sense, the time between the incarnation and the crucifixion/resurrection is the time for the bio-politics of the God without shelter, who nullified the inscription of the sovereign power upon his body. It is the experience of the messianic politics that exposes the *eschaton*—the 'time that remains,' and invokes the *Ekklesia* to the experience the bare-life—the state of exception—the crucifixion in which resurrection is embodied. As Achille Mbembe opines "the orgasmic power erected out of the flux of pain and the bio-salvatory energy sprout out of the wounds of the crucified body offers the radical memory of redemption today" (Mbembe, 2001: 235).

Unlike Western political theologians, whose theologies are founded on the notion of transcendence, theology of radical immanence locates transcendence within the possibility of the messianic irruption within it. It is here Agamben departs from the Christian political theologians of transformation that never envisages 'catastrophe' within it—the crucifixion or *kenosis*—the inoperativity of the sovereign power. For Christian political theologies, though it is separate and distinc: the immanent political realm is linked to a Transcendent God who is supposed to come from outside—Agamben calls it the 'providential' understanding of the *Oikonomia* (Agamben, 2007: 314). Agamben argues that it is through this transcendental logic, the capitalist-market discourses serve the role of liturgy today. Today the liturgical or the 'operation of glorification' is well performed by media as public praxis in the contemporary liberal world economy. Breaking of this liturgical continuity and experiencing the messianic politics is the function of the radical political theology of transformation.

Secondly, Christian theology has to become **Messianic politics.** Alluding to Walter Benjamin, Agamben argues that Theology has to become the messianic politics that is founded on the theological notion of the eruption of the messianic time. Critiquing the Western political theologies that substantiate the notion of a sovereign God as the center of the economy of life (*Oikonomia*), Agamben argues that in those political theologies the state of exception is accommodated within the economy of God and the theology of salvation is offered as the extension of the benevolent action of the sovereign God. In messianic politics, the state of exception—the bare-life—the living dead becomes a messianic time of interruption of the sovereignty where the legality of the life is nullified. Agamben here makes use of the Pauline term 'messianic time'—the time that remains—the time that is transfigured in it. It is not a time in between the ascension and *parousia,* rather it is the time that is fulfilled in itself. For Agamben, eschatology is not the end of time but the time of the end. In Agamben's notion of messianic time, one is invited to be drawn by the *eschaton*. Messianic time, for Agamben, is not one of apocalypse but of immediacy. Following Benjamin, Agamben affirms that "the paradigm for the understanding of the present is messianic time" (Agamben, 2012: 59).

For Agamben, Church is the called out community to live for this messianic politics. According to Agamben, to be called as a member of Church is to inoperate or de-activate or de-energize the effect of biopolitics of sovereignty and to be baptized by the spirituality of messianic politics. The Church—*Ekklesia*—embodies the hope of the tortured bodies and offers an eschatological community for those who have no community at all. To be called as a Church means to become a 'coming community', which lives in the (end) time that remains and to become a non-juridical establishment that runs on certain rules of life. While defining Church, Agamben contends: "Living in this time, experiencing this time, is thus not something that the Church can choose, or choose not, to do. It is only in this time that there is a Church at all" (Agamben, 2012: 13). It is this messianic politics that deactivates oneself from the dominant political program and identify with the marginalized and disenfranchised, which makes the Church a coming community. In short, the turn towards the messianic politics invokes the Church to become the crucified body of Jesus Christ to find itself in the state of exception; rather than offering salvation to the tortured bodies located 'outside' of its de-limited ontology through its diaconal/liturgical discourses.

Thirdly, Christian theology has to take a **poetical turn.** The poetical turn envisages theology as a creative engagement of all who sense the agony of life—the bare-life. Christian theology as *poiesis* overcomes the inherent problem of politicization of life and offers a pedagogy of embodied/enmattered/enfleshed salvation. Christian theology as *poiesis* nullifies its dogmatic rigidity and doctrinal fixity and becomes polydoxical in content where all the progressive forces join together to affirm the social ontology of salvation of all. It is in this pedagogy of *poiesis,* liturgy becomes political, sacramental becomes secular, and theology becomes *theopoiesis.* The methodology of *poiesis*, takes theological academia beyond the pedagogy of *praxis*, which de-limits theological program in dialectics as it is focused on the futuristic fulfillment in history (*telos*).

In *theopoiesis*, God is named as the poet by which it is refrained from defining God as a person, a force, a substance, a cosmic law, or even as a fixed concept. On the other hand, God is considered as a creative process of becoming of the creation from within. God is understood here as the ultimate novelty of creation or as the organic potentiality of creativity. According to this tradition, theologians are participants of the creative process of being, becoming, and belonging of the experience of planetarity. For them, theological is always epistemological, ontological, and political. While defining theology as *theopoiesis*, Sharon D. Welch exhorts theologians: "Let us be artisans, artisans of hope, artisans of wonder, working with human longing for generosity, courage, forgiveness, and resilience. As artisans, let us craft together flourishing communities of honesty, inclusion, justice, self-critique, and hope" (Faber & Fackenthal, 2013: 3).

Theology in this *theopoietic* sense becomes more creative (spontaneous, organic, and aesthetical), critical (encounter, interrogation, and prophetic), and imaginative (alluric, enigmatic, and apocalyptic). *Theopoiesis* is a process of being and becoming to be a part of the social ontology of salvation. Thus, doing theology in this *theopoietic* tradition is ontological in content as it invokes us to be part of the common ontology of redemption which is inherent within. The salvific experience is defined here as common, multiple and potential within. Here, the act of doing theology becomes embodied, enmattered, and immanent. Theology as *theopoiesis* envisages a polydoxical ground, through which it overcomes the binaries of secular/sacred, religion/politics, theism/atheism, spirit and matter, God and the world. As Catherine Keller alludes, theology in the contemporary context would uphold a "rhizomatic radicality" which is founded on a "polydoxic" philosophical/theoretical/religious inheritance. Keller contends that "such "rhizomatic radicality" is not about uprooting our traditions but about exposing them to our confounding togetherness—as species, peoples, genders, sexualities, races, religions, even—Lord help us—our Christianities" (Caputo & Keller, 2007: 108). Christianity, not only Christian theology, is invited here to validate the multiplicity of its being, becoming, and belonging in this planet earth.

Conclusion

The politics of redemption envisages three methodological re-imaginations: the turn towards immanence, the turn towards messianic politics, and becoming *theopoiesis*. Theological academia/ the Church has to take these epistemological contentions seriously in order to re-constitute itself as the discourse of the politics of redemption. The purpose of theological education is to invoke theological academia/ the Church to prepare ontologically and epistemologically to de-activate the biopolitics of the sovereign power inscribed upon them. The cruciform existence of the Church is not to sacrifice its life for the transformation of the society; rather to re-constitute itself as the state of exception—the bare-life and thereby become a salvatory experience for all. The role of theological education is to remind the Church to become *Ekklesia*—the tortured body of Christ as it signifies the political ontology of salvation for all. The politics of redemption is not just trans-formation based on the 'ethos of transcendence'; rather it is making the Church to get-ready for the inevitable catastrophe—the crucifixion in the world of the empire. As Arundhati Roy says, it is to listen to the grasshoppers—the 'nothings and the nobodies' of the world and learn how they resist the empire—the logic of sovereign state/God. Theological education here becomes *poiesis* by which theologians becomes artisans of hope, fraternity, and eternity.

References

Achille Mbembe, *On the Postcolony* (Berkeley: University of California Press, 2001).

Giorgio Agamben, *Homo Sacer: Sovereign Power and Bare Life*, trans. Daniel Heller-Roazen (Stanford: Stanford University Press, 1998).

Giorgio Agamben, *The Church and The Kingdom*, trans. Leland de Durantay, (London, New York, Calcutta: Seagull Books, 2012).

John D. Caputo & Catherine Keller, "Theopoiesis and theopolitics," *Crosscurrents*, Winter 2007, 105-11 at 108.

Mark Lewis Taylor, *The Theological and the Political: On the Weight of the World* (Minneapolis: Fortress Press, 2011).

Renee D. N. Riessen, "Community and its Other, Remarks on Giorgio Agamben's The Coming Community from Levinasian point of view," *Zeitschrift fur Dialektische Theologie,* Supplement Series 5, 2015.

Roland Faber & Jeremy Fackenthal,., "The Manifold of Theopoetics" Introduction, *Theopoetic Folds: Philosophizing Multifariousness,* (New York: Fordham University Press, 2013).

6

The Bio-Politics of the Crucified: Overcoming the Phenomenology of Violence*

Introduction

'Crucifixion was a profound event of violence' (Hengel, 1977). Does crucifixion of Jesus perpetuate violence? Was it an act of 'violence against the legitimized violence'? If not, how do we argue that it was a 'promise of the end of violence'? It was the atonement theories that attempted to address the issue of the 'scandal of the cross' in the history of the Church. Atonement theories denoted the notions of 'sacrifice,' 'propitiation,' 'satisfaction,' and 'vicarious suffering' to define the theological meaning of the crucifixion. However, there are theologians who believe that the atonement theories had legitimized violence in its relation with the sacred (Weaver, 2001; Kotsko, 2010l;

---

* Paper presented at the International Seminar on Biblical Response to Justice at UBS, Pune on 8-10th September, 2016.

Baker & Green, 2000). Exposing the violence of the atonement theories, the feminist theologians such as Rosemary Radford Reuther condemned on the 'satisfaction model' as "sadomasochistic theology and practice based on the idea of an 'offended' God who can only be mollified through the payment of innocent blood" (Reuther, 1998: 100). Hans Boersma contends that "without violence, the central act of salvation is unthinkable" (Boersma, 2006: 41).

The intersection between violence and sacred is expounded by many philosophers like Rene Girard and Gianni Vattimo, especially on the crucifixion of Jesus in the Roman imperial period (Gerard, 1996; Vattimo, 2003; Pallmeyer, 2003; Vries, 2002; Lifebure, 2000). Based on the theology of the cross, Vattimo offers a politics of *kenosis* or nihilism to overcome the inherent content of violence in religion (Vattimo, 2003). Girard's effort is to signify Jesus' crucifixion as the exposition of the inherent myth of 'scape-goat mechanism' in religion (Girard, 1987:10). However, the question of the violent death of Jesus on the cross and the myriad political victims in the world remain unresolved. How do we re-signify the violent death of Jesus as 'the promise of the end of violence'? How do we re-imagine the bio-politics of the crucified as the redemptive act of resistance of the tortured bodies in the contemporary global context of the empire? This paper tries to signify the violent death of Jesus on the cross as the bio-politics of the crucified people in the history, as Achille Mbembe re-defines cross, "where the orgasmic power erected out of the flux of pain becomes the bio-salvatory energy and the bodily implosion produced by his suffering becomes the radical memory of redemption" in the world of violence and violations (Mbembe, 2001: 235).

The bio-politics, as it is theorized by Michel Foucault designates what "brought life and its mechanisms into the realm of explicit calculations and made knowledge-power an agent of transformation of human life" (Foucault, 1979: 143). According to Foucault, bio-politics is the power of the body to de-inscribe the deployment of sovereign power upon it and exercise the productive capacity of the power to new life. Michael Hardt and Antonio Negri defined bio-politics as the power to constitute new political relations encompassing the individual life and prepares the ground for a revolutionary subject: *the multitude* in the context of the empire (Hardt & Negri, 2000: 405-6). Giorgio Agamben, on the other hand, argues that politics has always been bio-political by which the sovereign power of the state legally excludes or exercises its right to torture or kill the slaves, the refugees, the inhabitants of the camps, the immigrants, the unborn, the stateless (Agamben, 1998: 11). Agamben finds hope in the eruption of the 'messianic politics' as it was proposed by Walter Benjamin. However, Foucault, unlike Agamben, finds hope in the "technologies of self" that enable ourselves to be part of the resurrection of the "collective subjectivities"—*the multitude* (Hardt and Negri).

Achille Mbembe, by offering a revision in this argument of bio-politics, argues that the sovereignty deploys its power upon the vulnerable bodies based on some pre-figurative notions such as racism, which he termed as phenomenology of violence. The slave bodies carry some pre-figurative notions in terms of the phenomenology of racism, which make them entitled for killing. For Mbembe, unless and until we deconstruct this notion of the metaphysical violence embodied in the disposition of sovereignty upon human bodies we will not be able to challenge the politics of death (*necropolitics*) and find meaning in our collective bio-political resistance for redemption. Redemption, in this "social-relational" sense demands a "relational ontology" of salvation which denies the dichotomy between crucifixion and resurrection. Taking the cue of Achille Mbembe's theoretical framework on the phenomenology of violence on the slave bodies, this paper offers a theological appraisal of the redemptive bio-politics of the crucified Jesus and a critique of the atonement theories by following the liberative stream of feminists/womanists, Black, Dalit theologies of redemption which connects the bio-politics of the crucified Jesus with the political resistances of the countless victims in this world.

Deconstructing the Phenomenology of Violence: Achille Mbembe on the African 'Crucified' Slave Bodies

Achille Mbembe, the well-known African scholar elucidates his theory of phenomenology of violence by exposing the colonial composition of the 'slave bodies' in the European Slave trades. He explains:

> Who is a slave if not the person who, everywhere and always, possesses life, property, and body as if they were alien things? Possessing life and body as alien things presupposes that they are like external matter to the person who bears them, who serves as their scaffolding. In such case, the slave's body, life and work may be attacked. The violence thus perpetuated is not supposed to affect the slave directly, as something real and present. Thus, "slave" is a forename we must give to a man or woman, whose body can be degraded, whose life can be mutilated and whose work and resources can be squandered—with impunity. To someone who is a slave we can also give the forename "thing." By "thing" we understand the contrary of the substantive—that is something that somewhere is *nothing*. But the thing, like slave, is also that on which a person arrogates the right to exercise her or his will. As such, the thing does not determine itself at all. It is something that belongs to a person who happens, by chronology or by force, to be the first to take possession of and enjoy it (Mbembe, 2001: 235-6).

For Mbembe, the colonies are the best examples of the phenomenology of violence embodied in the common bond between the conqueror and the slave. In the eyes of the conqueror, the slave life is nothing but a savage life which has no validity to live. For the conqueror, these savage lives lack human character, thus there is nothing illegal to kill them for the program of progress or development. Alluding to Hannah Arendt, Mbembe clearly explicates this and writes, "the slaves are, as it were, "natural" human beings who lack the specifically human character, the specifically human reality, so that when European men massacred them they somehow were not aware that they had committed murder" (Mbembe: 12). Mbembe writes, "Because the slave's life is like a "thing," possessed by its master, the slave existence appears as a perfect figure of a shadow."

According to Mbembe, the crucial point of the phenomenology of violence is the shadowing of the slave body or the rejection of the materiality of the slave body.

Mbembe argues that the phenomenology of violence based on the notion of sovereignty pre-figurates the slave body and substantiates the physical torture embodied in it. For Mbembe, the biopolitics of the sovereignty functions on certain presupposed norms on terror, territory, and slave bodies. By defining the slave body as no-thing and non-being, the sovereign power legitimized the culture of violence in the European slave trades. According to Mbembe, thus, the central project of sovereignty is the generalized instrumentalization of human existence and the material destruction of human bodies and populations. Mbembe calls this *necropolitics*—the legally sanctioned politics of death.

Connecting this politics of death with the crucifixion of Jesus, Mbembe signifies a radical political theology of the crucified body. According to Mbembe, the death of Jesus does not involve a destructive drive alone; rather in it is embodied a mystery of salvation within. For Achille, the re-location of Jesus' body as the slave body on the cross in the Roman imperial context plays a salvatory role in the history of Christianity as it is clothed with the shadow of resurrection (Mbembe: 223). Mbembe says, "The body of the dead man on the cross is not reducible to its fundamental thingness. In fact, the figurative dimension is already there, poetic, clothed in appearance: the other face of the shadow" (Mbembe: 224).

According to Mbembe, the resurrection disclosed the thingness of the crucified body and elevated it into another form of being, beyond temporality—beyond the violence of death which had been the highest hope of the slaves in that period. Mbembe succinctly says that the crucifixion clothed in resurrection in the Roman imperial context decomposes the phenomenology of violence that imposes pain and agonies upon the crucified slave bodies. For him, 'the orgasmic power erected out of the flux of pain and the bio-salvatory energy sprout out of the wounds of the crucified body' offers the radical memory of redemption today (Mbembe: 235). Critically engaging with the atonement theories that perpetuated Jesus' death as a sacrificial one, Mbembe affirms the representative character of

Jesus' death in exposing the redemptive power of cross in the history of the bio-politics of the slave bodies everywhere in the world to overcome the phenomenology of violence.

Delineating the Bio-politics of the Crucified: Reading Bible for Overcoming the Phenomenology of Violence

The references of cross in the biblical texts are counter narratives through which it shows its political solidarity with the slave-lives in the Greco-Roman world. Cross was the most shameful capital punishment given to the slaves (*servile supplicium*) in the first century Roman imperial period. Cross was not only a mode of punishment in the first century Roman period; rather it was a legitimizing point out of which the sovereignty of the Roman empire was constructed. Slave-bodies are determined and inscribed by the sovereign power of the state and thus the crucified slave-bodies exhibit the bio-politics of the empire. On the contrary, the Bible, especially the gospels, try to bring out the counter-biopolitics of the crucified Jesus in terms of 'emptying out' (*kenosis*) of the bio-politics of the Roman sovereign power inscribed upon the slave-bodies.

The biblical scholars, who offer detailed studies on the formation of subjectivity in the first century Roman imperial context in the overall background of gospels, address this counter-political program of Jesus to de-possess or exorcise the enslaving subjectivity of the Roman citizens. According to Theodore W. Jennings, Jr. the gospel writers' intention was to picturize Jesus' martyrdom as an anti-imperial strategy (Jennings: 2003). As Wellborn rightly said, the Bible, especially the gospels, played a significant role to record the stories of the cruciform subjectivities of the people in the Greco-Roman world, especially the pathos of the slave lives which had been neglected by the prominent literatures of that period. Delving into ancient Greco-Roman literature, Welborn argues that the cross, which had been the haunting memory in the lower classes of the Roman Empire, got wide attention in the Bible while it was totally absent in the elite literature. Welborn writes:

> There are no references to the cross in learned Roman writers such as Lucretius, Virgil, Statius, or Aulus

> Gellius, and there is little or no mention of crucifixion in Greek writers such as Plutarch, Dio Chrysostom, Aelius Aristides, or maximus of Tyre. What is truly remarkable is the absence of the words *crux* and *patibulum* from the works of Caesar, despite the fact that he is known to have used crucifixion as punishment; the same is true of Pliny the younger, who as governor of Bithynia must have condemned many to the cross. Inevitably, there are differences to crucifixion in Greek and Roman historians who recount wars and rebellions, but even in such cases there is reticence and a tendency to portray crucifixion as a barbarian mode of execution. It is clear that the rarity of references to crucifixion in canonical literature is not an historical accident, but a reflection of the social and aesthetic values of upper-class writers (Welborn, 2013: 136-7).

This counteract is well-evident in Pauline epistles also. When Paul articulates his gospel as a "message about the cross" (1 Cor. 1: 18) he clearly explicates his solidarity with the lower classes of his period—"the nothings and nobodies"—the uneducated, poor, and low born (1 Cori. 1-26-28) of the country (Blanton & Vries, 2013: 134-5). As Welborn rightly said: "Paul claims that the purpose of God's intervention in history was not the liberation of a universal subject from the path of death, but rather the redemption of the many oppressed, whose identities are submerged in shame and whose lives are in danger of disappearing on account of the annihilating power of the cross" (Welborn 2013: 137). The annihilating power of the cross later becomes the "weak messianic power" (Walter Benjamin) for the weak and lowborn, which is expounded by Paul in 2 Corinthians:

> But we have this treasure in earthen vessels, so that it may be clear that this extraordinary power belongs to God and does not come from us. We are afflicted in every way, but not crushed; perplexed, but not driven to despair; persecuted, but not forsaken; struck down, but not destroyed; always carrying about in our body

> the mortification (*nekrosis*) of Jesus, in order that the life of Jesus may be manifest in our body. For constantly we the living are being handed over into death on account of Jesus, so that the life of Jesus may be manifest in our mortal flesh. (2 Cor. 4:7-11)

Despite some of the gospel texts that try to account Jesus' death on the cross as 'sacrificial death,' 'ransom for many,' 'sin-offering,' 'cleansing,' etc., the Pauline texts delineate it as the Christ-event. Invoking our participation in the Christ event, Paul writes: "For if we have been united with him in a death like his, we will certainly be united with him in a resurrection like his. We know that our old self was crucified with him so that the body of sin might be destroyed, and we might no longer be enslaved to sin. For whoever has died is freed from sin. But if we have died with Christ, we believe that we will also live with him" (Rom. 6: 5-8). As Paul argues in 1 Corinthians 1:26-31, we infer that the proclamation of the crucified Messiah summoned the weak and the low born into the material density of the cross, where Christ's willingness to suffer the very death that threatened their existence became the resource for living on in righteousness, sanctification, and redemption. Here, the proclamation of the crucifixion of Jesus and the participation in the Christ-event become the acts of the 'promise of hope' for the 'nothings and nobodies' of this world in the crucial context of the *necropolitics* of the empire.

The bio-politics of the crucified denies the deployment of power upon it. To challenge the sovereignty of the empire, the crucified body enunciates itself as a salvatory power for the 'nothings and the nobodies' and thus becomes the promise of hope. Unlike the atonement theories, it never sanctifies the suffering and unlike Mel Gibson's *Passion of the Christ* it never valourizes the bodily pain. As Girard contends, "there is nothing sacrificial about the death of Jesus on the cross. On the contrary, differentiating from the mythical concealing of violence, the biblical narrative exposes violence and helps make an end of the cycle. Indeed, Jesus 'dies' not as a sacrifice but in order that there may be no more sacrifices" (Girard, 1987: 180). According to Paul, participating in the Christ event through the sacraments is to invoke the *ekklesia* to be reminded of this bio-politics of the crucified bodies in this world. Bio-politics of the crucified Christ is enacted through the acts of 'brokenness' and thereby the eucharistic counter-communities become the embodiments of new humanity in the crucified Christ in the world of violence and domination.

The eruption of the new humanity exalts the cross as the promise of hope and thereby becomes the end of violence in history. As Walter Wink writes "the victory of the cross consists of the breaking the spirit of violence" (Wink, 1992: 109). Referring to Revelation 19, Miroslav Volf contends: "the end of the world is not violence, but a non-violent embrace without end. The world to come is ruled by the one who on the cross took violence upon himself, in order to conquer the enmity and embrace the enemy. The Lamb's rule is legitimized not by the sword but by its wounds" (Volf, 1990: 300-301). Volf concludes: "the scandal of the cross must remain, not as a way of affirming the legitimacy of violence, let alone abuse, but rather as a way to embrace the "promise of the cross: redemption, liberation, salvation and finally the end of violence" (Volf, 1990: 25).

The Lynched Black Bodies and the Tortured Dalit Bodies: Bio-politics of the Untouchable Bodies to Overcome the Phenomenology of Violence

"Dey carry him to Calvary and dey licked him wid violence" (Black Spirituals).

Connecting cross and the lynching in America, James H. Cone argues that the lynched Black victims experienced the same fate as the crucified Christ and thus became the most potent symbol for understanding the true meaning of salvation achieved through "God on the Cross" (Cone, 2011: 160). For him, the experiences of lynching were the marks of crucifixion inscribed on the American Black bodies. Lynching was an act of torturing Blacks in 1980s in America. It was a public activity in which the media announces the place, date and time of the expected hanging and burning of Black victims, and white communities gather to watch the killing. Cone explains this cruel act of lynching:

> It was a family affair, a ritual celebration of white supremacy, where women and children were often given the first opportunity to torture Black victims—burning Black flesh and cutting of genitals, fingers, toes, and ears as souvenirs. Postcards were made from the photographs taken of Black victims with white lynchers and onlookers smiling as they struck a pose for the camera. They were sold for ten to twenty-five cents to members of the crowd, who then mailed them to relatives and friends, often with a note saying something like this: "This is the barbeque we had the last night (Cone, 2011: 9).

Denying the atonement theory's emphasis on suffering, Cone affirms its salvatory content of the cross: "The theology of cross is not a rational concept to be explained in a theory of salvation, but a story about God's presence in Jesus' solidarity with the oppressed, which led to his death on cross. What is redemptive is the faith that God snatches victory out of defeat, life out of death, and hope out of despair, as revealed in the biblical and black proclamation of Jesus' resurrection" (Cone, 2011: 150). Interpreting the black spirituals, Copeland writes: "If the marks of the spirituals glorified in singing of the cross of Jesus, it was not because they were masochistic and enjoyed suffering. Rather, the enslaved Africans sang because they saw the result of the cross—triumph over the principalities and powers of death, triumph over evil in this world" (Cone 2011: 150-1). Cone reinstates it and expounds clearly the promise of hope embodied in the cross of Jesus Christ. He writes:

> The cross is the most empowering symbol of God's loving solidarity with the "least of these" the unwanted in society who suffer daily from great injustices: Christians must face the cross as the terrible tragedy it was and discover in it, through faith and repentance, the liberating joy of eternal salvation (Cone, 2011: 156).

The Dalit bodies in India also share the same agony of torturing and tormenting. Dalits, the former untouchables and the most tortured people in India embody the marks of rejection from the very beginning of the emergence of the Vedic phenomenology of caste. The phenomenology of caste is inherently violent as it perpetuates practices of othering and torturing, which is legally sanctioned by both (Vedic) religion and politics. Rohit Vemula, a Dalit PhD scholar at Hyderabad University who committed suicide due to the marginalization and seclusion he had experienced within the academy, wrote in his suicide note: "The value of a man was reduced to his immediate identity and nearest possibility. To a vote. To a number. To a thing. Never was a man treated as a mind. As a glorious thing made up of star dust. In every field, in studies, in streets, in politics and in dying and living" (Rohit Vemula's suicide note). Of course, caste is a system of *necropolitics* that entitles Dalit bodies for legalized killing and torture on the basis of a phenomenology of violence.

According to the National Commission for Scheduled Caste (NCSC), there had been an almost 40 per cent increase in the incidence of crime against Dalits in India in between 2011 and 2014. That means three cases per day! Despite the helplessness of Dalits in India, it does not force them to take a violent mode, which is well said by Ravi Sarvaiya, a survivor of torture against Dalits: "We are followers of Bhimarao Ambedkar who taught us non-violence. We are not like terrorists. Yet we took out a protest when they beat us mercilessly. We have to resort to drastic steps to make a point" (Katakam, 2016: 119). Ravi Sarvaiya's words reverberates with the non-violent mode of Dalit struggles in India to envisage a social democracy in India. The Dalit protest which has been unleashed with the suicide of Rohit Vemula has ignited a new momentum in Dalit politics in India. Arundhati Roy opines that Rohit Vemula will live in the Indian wounded psyche as a counter memory by challenging the *necropolitics* of elite nationalism and militant democracy (Roy, 2016: 49-67).

As Mark Heim highlights, normally in the religious myths, "The sacrificial one does not raise from the tomb but rather completely disappears in memory, so that the victim of sacrifice cannot be perceived as a victim" (Heim, 2006). However, the crucial narrative of the crucified in the Bible in the shadow of resurrection signifies counter memories of the tortured bodies today. The crucified Christ still continues to haunt us through. Rohit Vemulas and thus becomes the 'promise of the end of violence.' Like the crucified Christ in the Roman Empire, every tortured (Dalit) body in Indian return to the public society as a counter-memory of the end of violence. It is here the 'sacrifice' or 'giving oneself' for the cause of justice becomes the social ontology of salvation of all. Re-membering the crucified becomes the act of redemption when it is re-enacted, lamented and celebrated in the contemporary context of violence and violation. It is in these counter memories of the crucified people the promises of hope are embodied. It is in these bio-politics of the crucified people, the phenomenology of violence is unmasked and decomposed.

Conclusion

The crucified body pre-figurates the phenomenology of violence of the sovereign state and religion. However, the bio-politics of the crucified becomes the promise of hope as it envisions a crucified *multitude*—a collective subjectivity that resists the sovereign deployment of power on the tortured bodies. The tortured bodies are therefore inherently redemptive as they discharge the bio-salvatory energy erected out of the flux of pain and the bodily implosion of suffering. Crucified body as the site of salvation offers a radical ontology of relationality which overcomes the dichotomy between crucifixion and resurrection. The redemptive act of the crucified body or its non-violent embodiment lies in the doxological act of the counter-eucharistic communities. It is here the bio-politics of the crucified becomes the Christ-event that invokes us to participate in it for envisaging a non-violent social order. In sum, the crucified body which is tortured on the basis of the phenomenology of violence becomes the promise of hope in the contemporary world of violence through its inherent bio-politics of redemption. The crucified body, whether it is a dalit body, slave body, black body, woman body, or no-body, the tortured body is not reduced to its thingness; but the poetic/ politics of redemption is clothed within it as a shadow. Arundhati Roy is so poetic (of course political too) when she signifies Rohit Vemula as the spirit that haunts the Indian republic today (Roy, 2006: 69). Overcoming violence in the contemporary context of the empire is to find hope in the redemptive bio-politics of the tortured bodies as it is envisaging the social democracy of *the multitude.*

References

Achille Mbembe, *On the Postcolony* (London: University of California press, 2001).

Achille Mbembe, *Necropolitics,* Public Culture 15 (1): 12.

Adam Kotsko, *The Politics of Redemption: The Social Logic of Salvation* (London: T&T Clark, 2010).

Anupama Katakam, Torture and Backlash, *Frontline,* August 19, 2016, 117-121.

Arundhati Roy, My Seditious Heart: An Unfinished diary of nowadays, *The Caravan* May 2016.

Denny J. Weaver, *Non-violent Atonement* (Grand Rapids: Eerdmans, 2001).

Gianni Vattimo, *Nihilism & Emancipation: Ethics, Politics, and Law* (New York: Columbia University Press, 2003).

Giorgio Agamben, *Homo Sacer: Sovereign Power and Bare Life,* trans. Daniel Heller-Roazen (Stanford: Stanford University Press, 1998).

Hans Boersma, *Violence, Hospitality and the Cross: Re-appropriating the Atonement Traditions* (Grand Rapids: Baker Academics, 2006).

Hent de Vries, *Religion and Violence: Philosophical Prospects from Kant to Derrida* (Baltimore: John Hopkins University Press, 2002).

Jack Nelson-Pallmeyer, *Is Religion Killing Us? Violence in the Bible and the Quran* (Harrisburg, Pa.: Trinity Press International, 2003).

James H. Cone, *The Cross and the Lynching Tree* (Maryknoll, New York: Orbis Books, 2011).

Leo D. Lifebure, *Revelation, the Religions and Violence* (Maryknoll, NY: Orbis, 2000).

L.L. Welborn, "The Culture of Crucifixion and the Resurrection of the Dispossessed: The Interpellation of the Subject in the Roman Empire and Paul's Gospel as "Truth Event" in Ward Blanton & Hent De Vries, eds., *Paul and the Philosophers* (New York: Fordham University Press, 2013).

Mark Heim, *Saved from Sacrifice: A Theory of the Cross* (Grand Rapids: Eerdmans, 2006).

Martin Hengel, *Crucifixion in the Ancient World and the Folly of the Message of the Cross* (Philadelphia: Fortress, 1977).

Mark D. Baker and Joel B Green, *Recovering the Scandal of Cross: Atonement in New Testament and Contemporary Contexts* (Owners, III: InterVarsity Press, 2000).

Michel Foucault, *The History of Sexuality, vol.1. An Introduction* (London: Allen Lane, 1979).

Michael Hardt and Antonio Negri, *Empire* (Cambridge, MA/London: Harvard University Press, 2000).

Miroslav Volf, *Exclusion and Embrace: A Theological Exploration of Identity, otherness and reconciliation* (Nashville: Abingdon, 1990).

Rene Girard, *Things Hidden Since the Foundation of the World*, trans. Stephen Bann and Michael Matteer (Stanford, California: Stanford Press, 1987).

Rene Girard, *The Girard Reader* edited by James G. William (New York: the Cross Road, 1996).

Rosemary Radford Reuther, *Introducing Redemption in Christian Feminism*, Introductions in Feminist Theology I (Sheffield: Sheffield Academic Press, 1998).

Theodore W. Jennings, *Insurrection of the Crucified: The Gospel of Mark as Theological Manifesto* (Chicago, Il: Exploration Press, 2003).

Walter Wink, *Engaging the Powers: Discernment and Resistance in a World of Domination. The Powers 3* (Minneapolis: Fortress, 1992).

Ward Blanton & Hent De Vries, eds., Paul and the Philosophers (New York: Fordham University Press, 2013).

7

Reconstituting a Theology of Multitude in India*

Introduction

As a pioneering ecumenical institution in India, the role of the Christian Institute for the Study of Religion and Society (CISRS) in enabling the churches in India to participate in nation building can never be neglected. It was through CISRS, Indian Christian theologians such as P. D. Devanandan and M. M. Thomas initiated various researches and social action programmes to inspire the Indian churches to involve in social emancipation practices. This year, CISRS offers a platform for Indian Church leaders to discuss the contemporary challenges of democracy and politics in India in connection with the centenary celebrations of Dr. M. M. Thomas. In the process of formulating a contemporary political theology in India, this national consultation would like to attend the metamorphosis

* Key-note address at the National Consultation on *Resisting the Empire: Re-imagining Multitudes* on 11 August, 2015, at YMCA, New Delhi.

happening to contemporary politics, democracy, and state in the contemporary age of the empire. It is not a coincidence that we celebrate M. M. Thomas' centenary this year in the wake of the 40th anniversary of the declaration of the internal emergency in India.

Responding to the state of emergency declared at the midnight of June 25-26, 1975, Thomas said: "It is nothing but the onslaught on democracy and a betrayal of the nation." Rejecting Mrs. Gandhi's claims for the declaration of the emergency, Thomas argued that unless we support the revolts resulting from the people's efforts to throw off the age-old socio-cultural and economic exploitative structures, the issues of poverty, economic backwardness, and political instability will remain with us forever (2000: 30). For Thomas, the economic progress of the nation is integrally connected to the issues of caste, patriarchy, and slavery. Thomas contended that the effort to quieten the people's revolts for the sake internal peace, economic progress, and self-reliance through the state of emergency, is nothing but the repudiation of all human rights envisaged by welfare state and its democracy (49). Thomas' observation is right as he analyzes, it was the emergency in India that gave the impression to the multi-national corporates in the subsequent period that India can easily be purchased. The post-emergency economic policies testify to this fact. Today, when internal and external multi-nationals come to the local farmers of Indian villages to grab their farming land and the people's resistances to this 'state sponsored terrorism' are reckoned as anti-state, anti-democratic, and anarchic, we need to uphold what Thomas once said: "We need a political spirituality that keeps us always in opposition."

While defending the role of the people's constitution that enhances people's mobilization for social justice, Thomas once warned: "Any constitution or any system can become an instrument of vested interests insofar as it does not emerge as a result of process in which the people are mobilized for social justice" (89). In this logic of democracy, the state of emergency still continues in our country. When the people's resistances to the contemporary hegemonic governance are counted as anti-democratic and unconstitutional, it is imperative to define what constitutional democracy is and what it means when all the human rights are at stake. Constitutional, as

Thomas highlights, is nothing but being and becoming submissive to the sovereign laws and policies that legitimize the hegemony of the corporates over the common people, and thereby it reinstates its political process of exclusion of the weaker sections (91).

In the contemporary Indian political context, where we see Narendra Modi's strategy to incorporate the development dreams of the Indian elite with the multinational corporates, democracy assumes the global stature and the national citizens become trans-national subjects which demand new analytical tools to assess the metamorphosis happening to post-globalized Indian state and democracy. Yoga, which never has been a political resort to challenge the casteist, patriarchal, and the elitist social setting in India now has been projected as the mantra of global peace and unity. It is being done in the political context when beef-eating is banned and indigenous cultural pieces are saffronized. "The possibility of emergency is not yet devoid from us." It was the warning given by a veteran BJP leader recently. Of course, the legacy of emergency is still recurrent in Indian political discourses. Looking at the abandonment of human rights and the state sponsored violence against farmers and the weaker sections, the people's movements share the concern of the BJP leader about the impending doom of democracy in India today.

In the contemporary post-globalized era, as the sovereignty of the nation-states has been declined and at the same time it has been taken a form of a 'global governance,' the metamorphosis happening to the concepts of people, state, and democracy is to be addressed and analyzed seriously. How the state retains its sovereignty in connection with the global corporates and in what way the government legitimizes its power through its biopolitics are very significant questions in the process of defining democracy today. Does the right-endowed citizen and her socio-political mobilization today justify the modern concepts of 'people' and 'politics' as they were theorized in the modern Western liberal or the Marxist epistemological framework? In other words, is the liberal democratic or the Marxist concept of political mobilization and democracy still valid and significant in deconstructing the biopolitical formations of the people? Are the social movements capable enough to challenge the biopolitics of the sovereign state at it assumes multiple origins and micro-formations in the contemporary globalized context? How do we define politics when the micro-effects of the 'governmentality' are extended to even our human bodies? What would be a relevant political theology in India in the context of 'global governance' and its subsequent legitimization of the project of exclusion?

Addressing the imperative to envisage a 'life in common' in the contemporary context of 'global governance'—empire, Antonio Negri, the Italian philosopher (with Michael Hardt) offers a project of alternative global living—Multitude. Multitude is a global form of democracy over against the sovereign global order—empire (2004: xii). The project of Multitude demands an open and inclusive democratic global society that internally nullifies the project of empire. The empire today is not like the medieval/modern imperialism; rather it is a 'network power' that includes the dominant nation-states, trans-national institutions, capitalist corporations and other powers. Not all powers are equal in this power network. It is a system of inequality and hierarchies. However, all partners in this system maintain the order intact to keep up their position within. The empire exists by creating the state of war–state of conflict—within and without. War in empire is not a military action; rather it is the biopolitical act of "producing and reproducing" of the subjects (13). Negri and Hardt claim therefore that when "life itself is put on center stage, then *war becomes properly ontological* (19)". It is this ontological war situation that sanctions the suspension of the democracy.

According to Negri, multitude is the living alternative that grows within the empire. In Negri's perspective, there are two types of globalization: (1) empire spreads globally its network of hierarchies and divisions that maintain order through new mechanisms of control and constant conflict; (2) new circuits of cooperation and collaboration that stretch across nations and continents and allow an unlimited number of encounters (xiii). This is the possibility to live in common and act together while we remain different. For Negri, multitude is an open net work—life in common. Common is not homogeneity, but alterity and difference. Unlike the concept of people, which is unitary and identitarian, multitude is many (xiv). Multitude is composed of many 'irreducible singularities' of cultures, races, ethnicities, genders, and sexual orientations. Multitude is many-colored. It goes beyond the category of class. Working class refers to all waged workers, separating them from the poor, unpaid domestic laborers, all the traditional workers who do not receive a wage. Rather, multitude is an inclusive concept. The multitude is thus a composed potentiality of all the diverse agents of social production. In the democracy of multitude, the economic, cultural, and the social realms enacte together to envisage an alternative life in common. Multitude offers a political ontology where the production of subjectivities is de-imperialized. For Negri, our struggles determine our subjectivities (197). It is the possibility to envisage a political democracy of 'common' in the age of empire.

The context of *resisting the empire and re-imagining* multitude in India demand a radical shift in the formulation of political theology in India. How do we do politics when we, ourselves are part of the ontology of the empire? How does the empire accommodate the resistances against it within? How does the Church response to this situation? Where do the churches in India stand? How does Christian theology 'inoperate' or 'de-energize' the imperial ontological constitution of the Church and Christianity? Modern political theologies have always been the liturgies of the sovereign God, who legitimizes "the imperio-colonial sense" of the West and the sovereignty of the modern state. This is evident in the Hobbesian political theory of state and the theology of God. Along with Hardt and Negri, the contemporary political thinkers Gianni Vattimo, Gilles Deleuze, Giorgio Agamben, Jean-Luc Nancy, Judith Butler, and Achille Mbembe demands the deconstruction of Christianity and envision a God after the death of god. It was M. M. Thomas who proposed a political theology of the crucified God—a God who denies its own sovereign ontology to nullify the rule of the Roman Empire—in the postcolonial Indian context.

According to Thomas, the cross is the self-manifestation of the self-forgetting and self-sacrificing God. Crucified one is the negation of the totalitarian exercise of power over humans. The empire is defeated and nullified on the cross. Cross signifies the end of the totalitarian power of either God or the state and the beginning of a new community—kingdom community—a universal community where there are no dichotomies. In the new community, "there is no longer any distinction between Gentiles and Jews, circumcised and uncircumcised, barbarians, savages, slaves, and free" (Col. 3:11). The new human community is constituted as a single body—the body of the crucified God in history. The crucified body of God is not a new thing; rather it is the body of the slain Lamb from the creation of the world and it continues to be slain till the end of the world, pre-figuring all political victims in this world. The mark of crucifixion continues to be the sign of the suffering struggle of God against the principalities and powers till the end of the world. It is a radical reconstitution of the political subjectivity through which the imperialist biopolitics is crucified and initiates a new ontology of solidarity and multiplicity. According to Thomas, the mission of the Church today is to embody this mark of crucifixion and thereby reconstitute its own ontology by baptizing it in the cry of the political victims in India today. Signifying M. M. Thomas, there is an imperative for the churches in India to reconstitute a political theology of multitude in India in order to witness the crucified God in India today.

References

Michael Hardt and Antonio Negri, *Empire (*Cambridge, MA: Harvard University Press, 2000).

Michael Hardt and Antonio Negri, *Multitude: War and Democracy in the Age of Empire* (New York: Penguin Press, 2004).

Michael Hardt and Antonio Negri, *Common Wealth* (Cambridge, MA: Harvard University Press, 2009).

M. M. Thomas, *Response to Tyranny* (Tiruvalla: CSS, 2000).

M. M. Thomas, *Crucified Jesus: The Lord of the World* (Tiruvalla: CSS & BTTBPSA, 2008).

P. D. Devanandan and M. M. Thomas, *India's Quest for Democracy* (Calcutta: YMCA Publishing House, 1955).

8

Towards a Planetary Christian Ethics in India*

Introduction

Nature is my God. If we don't love Nature, we cannot love humans.
Kallel Pokkudan, a dalit eco-political activist.

The glory of God is the human being fully alive.
Irenaeus of Lyons, Against Heresies

There was never a time when human agency was anything other than an interfolding network of humanity and nonhumanity; today this mingling becomes harder to ignore.
Jane Bennett, Vibrant Matter

Christian ethics has been founded on certain theological/philosophical notions of God and the other. How does humanity

---

* Key-note address in the National Consultation on *Theology, Ethics and Social Analysis: Contemporary Methodological Concerns*, organized by BTESSC, at UTC on 30-31st July, 2015.

relate to God and the other? What would be the rationale for the inter-human relationship as they are destined to be in community? How do we define our humanness in relation with the 'other,' the 'Wholly Other,' and mother earth? These are questions that have been pertinent in Christian ethics. Since ethics is integrally connected to theology, anthropology, and ecology, any attempt to analyze the contemporary ethics necessitates a method of multi-disciplinarity (Tracy, 1994: 3). On the more, the epistemological shifts in the understanding of God, humanness and Nature necessitates a deconstruction of the Christian ethics, as it was founded on the modern Western enlightenment epistemology.

Post-enlightenment ethics can be termed as 'ethics without ethics' or 'ethics after the death of God.' God as the Absolute point of determining all duties and obligation to the 'other' was challenged in postmodernity and thereby opened up a new context of non-foundationalism. In addition to this, the emergence of postcoloniality that interrogated the Eurocentric logic of 'totality' and its program of 'othering' made the contemporary ethics more complex and compound. The subaltern epistemologies that always have had a critical engagement with the hegemonic power structures and practices are still vibrant with their resistances for reclaiming their democratic (human) bodies and social bodies, demanding a radical logic of political ontology and social agency. Some of the post-ecological concerns offer a 'planetary ethics' through which they offer a political ontology of relationality and a materialist theology of becoming. In the contemporary world of empire where we are scattered and fragmented, the contemporary Christian ethics demands the 'interfolding network of humanity and nonhumanity' or the 'multifariousness of our being and becoming' (Roland Faber, *Theopoetic folds: Philosophizing Multifariousness*) which has become harder to neglect today.

Alluding to these epistemological challenges, this paper explores the possibility of constructing a contemporary ethics of political ontology and materialist theology in India engaging with some of the postcolonial/subaltern epistemologies as they uphold knowledges and practices of becoming and belonging human. It is an ethical thinking that fosters relationality and alterity, which helps us to get-rid of the baggage of essentialism and the fixity of locations. This paper offers a critical analysis on the methodological transitions in the discipline of Christian ethics as it tries to define the relationship between God and the other. To offer a contemporary method of doing Christian ethics in India, this paper tries to adopt a radical epistemology and ontology, which may help us to reimagine ourselves as posthumans. Here, Christian ethics reconstitutes itself as a public discourse that re-inscribes the story of a 'common life'—Multitude (as Gilles Deleuze calls it) and thereby bypass our dichotomies such as self/other; subject/object; mind/body; human/nonhuman; secular/sacred; state/people; religion/science; liturgy/politics; and theology/philosophy.

Christian Ethics: Methodologies in Transition

Ethics as a guild discipline is a modern Western program. It was the modern Western enlightenment epistemology that framed a systematic/scientific method for modern ethical thinking. In the pre-modern period, ethics was set in a mystical/symbolic world view legitimized by the fixed, universal, natural laws. The social relations and the structures were pre-destined and pre-determined. It is well evident in the Platonic-Aristotelian ethical principles on the slave-master relationship. The fixity of the social relationships and their legitimizing philosophical thoughts impacted heavily both the patristic and medieval theologies. The epistemological foundation of this world view had a very clear theological notion of God who is transcendently present in the process of ethical functioning of the society. Whether it was Aristotle or Thomas Aquinas there is a notion of God who operates within ethical relationships as an extrinsic force. It is clear that there is a transcendental notion of the relationship between God and the other that has become foundational for Christian ethics to define and determine the morality of the inter-human relationship since the formation of ethics as a guild discipline.

The 'God and the other' relationship in the modern Western philosophy/theology was founded on an absolutist and totalitarian notion of Being/God. Rene Descartes held the view that God exists as an innate 'infinitist thought' available to human mind and reason. In this totalitarian notion of God/Being/(European) self, 'the other'—the non-white-male-European is integrated within. This totalitarian ontology denied the alterity (difference) of 'the other.' For Descartes, 'the other' is nothing but an object of his thinking. Kant, on the other hand, offered a revision to the Cartesian philosophy and rehabilitated God as the universal moral idea that regulates all human experiences within the extension of 'phenomenon'. In the universalizing and unifying Kantian approach, 'the other' is only taken into consideration in a negative way. Gabrielle Hiltmann calls the Kantian approach a monistic and universal rationalist logic which excludes the positive recognition of the other's individuality (Hiltman, 2007:1); whereas Hegel held the view that God exists as an absolute self-conscious spirit (*Geist*) within the dialecticality of human consciousness. In the Hegelian thesis of negation which ultimately leads to wholeness—the many belong to the One—nullified the existence of 'the other' in the dialectical process of history. Taking a cue from Hegelian negative dialectics, the Frankfurt School—Adorno, Horkheimer, Benjamin, and Habermas—held the view that it is in this negative dialectics, the binarism between self and other, sacred and secular, theory and theology, thinking and doing are re-imagined and reconciled (Ott, 2006: 143). Here, the problem of God and the other is solved in a dialectical method.

It was Frederic Nietzsche who denied the modern Western totalitarian notion of God who stands as the ground of all universal claims of truth. By arguing for the 'death of God,' he rejected the modern idea of God as the universal center of all human values and life. In Nietzsche, God as "the super Being," "the absolute Truth," and the "absolute Goodness" came to an end. It was a clear rejection of the monotheistic, monadic, and unifying modern Western notion of God, beginning from Descartes, through Kant to Hegel. This rejection of the modern metaphysics and *onto-theology* accentuated the emergence of postmodern ethics, where the postcolonial world began to engage with social theories such as the Lyotard's critique of 'metanarratives,' the Foucauldian theory of the insurrection of the 'contested epistemologies,' and the Derridean method of 'deconstruction.'

i. Transcendental Ethics: Emmanuel Levinas

Nietzsche's critique of Oneness and the Heideggerian philosophy of ontological difference accentuated the process of dismantling the western idea of totality in the postmodern period. Heidegger's de-ontological God and the other were brought to the ethico-political realm by the philosophers of the 'new phenomenology': Emmanuel Levinas, Jacques Derrida, Jean-Luc Marion and so on, who offered the irreducible singularity of God/Other in contrast to the modern Western theistic, monistic, totalitarian philosophy of God. God as the 'transcendent Other' shifts radically from the Western onto-theology and attends to the postmodern question of the Other as a parallel to it. The Other in the postmodern context denies any kind of 'othering' and locates itself in a 'location' of alterity and irreducible singularity.

Emmanuel Levinas was one of the major proponents of postmodern ethics. According to Levinas, modernity is the logic of Euro-centric-totality that determines the subjectivity of its other (Levinas, 1969: 4-5). The radical otherness of the other is denied here and at the same time it is being defined on the logic of a sameness and universality. As Levinas highlights in modernity 'the other becomes objectified, while the subject remains the same.' The objectification of the other is not just an epistemological issue; rather, it is an act of terror on their bodies and souls. Levinas provokes us to feel the horrors of the Holocaust. In order to challenge the notion of totality, Levinas brings the notion of transcendence into the ethical relationship between the self and the other so that the self cannot accommodate the other within the logic of sameness. Levinasian ethics is called 'transcendental ethics' where the exterior location of the other determines its alterity. The other is the absolute Other—the radical Other—the enigmatic Other, which cannot be comprehensible and reducible. The problem with the Levinasian Other is that it is located at the fixed social location–the poor, the orphan, the widow and the destitute. This fixation of the other, even though it is capable enough to question the self, faces severe criticisms. Contrary to modern Western metaphysics and ontology, the inclusion of the other in Levinasian ethics is in the mode transcendence or the charity oriented love of the self to 'the other.' The other still has to wait for the 'sacrificial love' of the (European/colonial) self.

Sarah Ahmed argues that Levinas fails to address the social structure that determines the positioning or subjectivity of 'the other'—the poor, the widow, the orphan and the destitute (Ahmed 2000: 142). Ahmed contends that in Levinasian ethics there are two human beings: beings and alien beings. The alien beings are transcendent. Ahmed asks what the use of this 'transcendental ethics' is if the exclusive structure remains unchallenged. Why do we need ethics based on the charity oriented love of the self to the other? Judith Butler goes one step further and asks why does this Levinasian idea of transcendence become absent at the face of the people at Gaza who experience death every moment of their life (Butler points to the strategic silence of Levinas—the Lithuanian Jew—on the issue of Palestine) (Butler, 2012: 58). The Levinasian ethics, despite its capacity go beyond the modern Euro-centric ethics lacks the ability to address the day-to-day political experiences of marginalization and torture on the 'colonized bodies.' The postmodern theology, liturgy and ethics which find their foundation in this 'transcendental ethics' face interrogations today.

ii. The Liberation Ethics: Enrique Dussel

Latin American philosophers engaged with the postmodern philosophy to launch a liberation ethics, taking Latin America as a social location. Eduardo Mendieta—the Latin American philosopher—argues that modernity mirrored certain notions of universality, totality, and sovereignty and imposed this logic of transcendence over against the particular human experiences in the postcolonial world such as Latin America (Mendieta, 2003). As Homi Bhabha asks, "What is modernity in these colonial conditions where its imposition is itself the denial of historical freedom, civic autonomy and the 'ethical' choice of refashioning?" (Bhabha, 1994: 41). The Latin American liberation philosophers argue that the philosophy of liberation is "postmodern" as it offers the critique of modernity, although they prefer the term "trans-modern" (Dussel, 2003: 81).

However, the inadequacy of the postmodern philosophy to attend the issues of the 'colonized beings' (Enrique Dussel) made them to look at the critical theories of Frankfurt School, which tried to open up the Hegelian/Marxian ontology in terms of the dialectical process of 'negation of the negation.' Thus, liberation theologians were able to add a revision to the postmodern transcendental ethics by redefining transcendence as liberation instead of separation and exteriority. For them, the other is not an exterior other or the absolute other; rather it shares a relationality of liberation (relative transcendence)—a revolutionary praxis in relation with the self. The site of the other, whether it is the exploited laborer or the peripheral nation, is at the location of liberation as it dismantles the whole system of Capitalism—the product of modern metaphysics and ontology. History is the site of transcendence where God is present as an internal potentiality of freedom and justice. To participate in this internal transcendence (praxis) evokes liberation in history.

It was Enrique Dussel who crafted a systematic framework for liberation ethics. Alluding to Levinas, Dussel contends that modernity is a colonial project of totality that existed by legitimizing its other—Latin America. According to Dussel, Europe and America did not pre-exist colonial confrontation, but emerged out of it as an essential element of modernity. "By controlling, conquering, and violating the Other, Europe defined itself as discoverer, conquistador, and colonizer of an alterity likewise constitutive of modernity." Liberation ethics criticizes the unethical slave/master model ethics that legitimizes the determination of the master. According to Dussel, capitalism rests on the de-sublimating and mobilizing of human capacities for selfish violence. Capitalism produces excluded people and the dehumanized others—the poor labourer and the peripheral nations. Both of them are the victims of this 'colonization of being.' Dussel's liberation ethics is directed at restoring the humanity of the poor labourer and the peripheral nations that requires "the creation of ethical communities, that is, communities without the exploitation of labour, the destruction of the earth, and the systematic production of poverty, malnutrition, and famine" (Dussel, 2003: 83).

The difficulties in the liberation ethics disclose serious deficiencies in connection with the fixity of the subjectivity of the other as we see in the case of the Levinasian transcendental ethics. The other is still in the exteriority—in the transcendence—even though it is connected to the self in terms of the praxis. Though there is a process of dia-lectics (the praxiological relationship), the other accepts the totalitarian system that subordinates or excludes it. The alterity of the other or the liberation of the other is entangled somehow to the existence of the system, if not negatively. There is no 'irreducible singularity' for the poor and the peripheral nations without the system of exclusion. Here, the other always bears some fixed social locations or essentialist baggage even though it resists. Theoretical speaking, are there any 'multifarious' subject positions or incarnations (Catherine Malabou calls it *plasticity*) in the praxis-oriented dia (two)-lectical relationship between the self and the other? Is there any notion of human, God, and nature that exceeds the dialectical positional fixities and affirm a intersubjectivity–a radical ontology of being and becoming? The liberation ethics in India, whether it is the *contextual ethics* of K. C. Abraham or the *grassroots earth ethics* of George Zachariah or the *Dalithos* of Peniel Jesudasan Rufus Rajkumar, is not devoid of these epistemological trajectories (Abraham, 2006; Zachariah, 2011).

1. Towards a Planetary Christian Ethics in India

Whether it is postmodern ethics or liberation ethics, Christian ethics has always been transcendental in content. It legitimized the space or the role of the 'transcendent God', whether it is extrinsic or intrinsic. The postcolonial studies identify this space of transcendence as the space of colonialism to enter into it and determine the subjectivity of the other, whether it is the human other or the earth other. This epistemological dilemma demands a radical ontology and politics as it overcomes the inherent dialecticality between matter/spirit, body/mind, self/other, religion/science, theology/philosophy in the Western philosophy. The category—Western philosophy is used here not as a binary opposite of Eastern philosophy or Indian philosophy. Whether it is Western or Eastern or Indian, the philosophy that politically substantiates the power structures such as capitalism, caste, patriarchy, and hierarchy is not all useful for a radical Christian ethics in India. The unitarian-non-dualist-monistic philosophies in India have never been useful for formulating a radical political ontology, if not we deconstruct them otherwise. On the other hand, the use of subaltern epistemologies to formulate the grassroots ethics in India, as we see in the work of George Zachariah, does not overcome the problem of locating them in the position of 'the oppositional gaze' (Zachariah, 2011: 96-130). Thus, anything that is contributive to the construction of the notion of the inter-related humanity or a radical ontology of relationality, whether it is philosophy, science, social theories/stories, theologies, are significant for formulating the contemporary Christian ethics in India.

Gayatri Chakravorty Spivak, the postcolonial-feminist, offers a theory of planetarity, through which she tries to propose a 'detranscendentalized ethics.' Planetarity is a theory of a radical ontology of relativity where the planet becomes a place of alterity. The subaltern—the subordinated other—whether it is the human other or the earth other is an 'im/possible' location that overcomes any kind of 'othering.' It is a de-othered space—a postcolonial space. Like subalternity, planetarity is also a space of alterity. Planetarity is to 'counter act the global reach of capital' that overlooks our differences, and it accommodates subaltern humanity and the subaltern earth at the location of 'the other.' Whereas globalization is the imposition of sameness over the face of the planet, planetary is a way to think about how we are codefined and come together because of, with, and through our differences. "The planet is in the species of alterity, belonging to another; and yet we inhabit it, on loan." She further says that 'it belongs to another system-a system that is beyond our grasp as it is the inside of our bodies." Ritu Birla explains the notion clearly: "The planet, unlike the world, is a conceptual metaphor infused with the possibility of seeing from outside, of seeing from the perspective of the alien, and not merely of apprehending the unified sphere that is familiar to us from prominent discourses of absolute oversight" (Birla, 2010: 88).

Spivak asserts that the globe in which we live is a manageable world where we are successful and comfortable in showing love to our 'others.' On the other hand, 'planetary love' is not love for the other; rather, it is an experience of the 'deconstructive embrace' where both the self and other invent for their new incarnations.

Planetarity is a mentality in which we re-visit the constitutive other and the self in the context of globalization and envisage a 'radical relationality' that extends to the whole system of life on the planet. She continues: "if we imagine ourselves as planetary subjects rather than global agents, planetary creatures rather than global entities, alterity remains underived from us. This is as close to the sacred, again, as I come" (Spivak, 2011: 62).

As Kwok Pui-lan contends, planetarity is an invitation to imagine the complexity and plurality of planetary systems and not be confined by narrow identity politics or superficial binary thinking. Contrary to some of the Indian indigenous earth ethics, it is not an ecological exhortation or a theological/ethical reminder of our stewardship (Longchar: 2012). A planetary ethics thus calls for the experience of the impossible—detranscendelized sacred—that is radically open-ended. Instead of God, Spivak here uses the word –'planet' where we experience the 'detranscendelized sacred' and the 'deconstructive embrace.' It is in this planetarity the irreducibility and relationality are affirmed and experienced. It is in this 'deconstructive embrace' the other is de-othered and both the self and other go through the process of 'essentialization to trial' (Roland Faber). This 'radical love' is not simply an obligation to the 'other' as it is theologized by religions: "love your neighbor" and by human rights activists: "solidarity with the other". It is to experience "inter-carnations" in the political process of becoming human and belonging the earth.

The Spivakian planetarity is an invitation to live in an enigmatic relationship with the other, God, and the earth. The Spivakian detranscendelized sacred provides a vision of a relational, embodied, and sensible God that goes beyond the Western, theistic onto-theology of God. It falls on the 'plane of immanence,' in the process of constructing a materialist theology of God and political ontology of relationality. As Jea Sophia Oh argues, Spivakian planetarity comes to us as a call for responsibility (Oh, 2011: 79). It is not one of romantic imagination but one that reflects the ethical practice of human beings as planetary subjects. Spivak, who signifies the planet as God, defines planetarity as religiosity or dharma. The Spivakian God here locates itself beyond any kind of anthropomorphism of the divine or theo-morphism of the human. Developing this de-ontological notion of God, Mayra (Rivera proposes a theology of Holy Ghost, through which it is re-imagined as a theological figure that touches us with the haunting memories of human history in terms of the "ghostly encounters" of the victims Rivera, 2007: 129). For Ambedkar, it is the Dhamma, which is devoid of any sanction from an Absolute God, and enhances the political becoming of the marginalized, signifying a radical political ontology in India (Vinayaraj, 2015: 35-49).

Planetarity informs us about the interconnectivity between humanity and non-humanity. It is to re-imagine our identity and agency as a multiple site of the process of our becoming and belonging. While constructing a materialist political ontology, Jane Bennett contends that "human agency is always an assemblage of microbes, animals, plants, metals, chemicals, word-sounds, and the like—indeed, that is an agentic assemblage" (Bennett, 2010: 121). This radical vision of 'agentic assemblage' enhances us to see the gender/transgender issue differently. It is here we try to become posthumans. As Deleuze rightly explains the condition of posthuman, "the human becomes more than itself, or expands to its highest power, not by affirming its humanity, nor by returning to animal state, but by becoming-hybrid with what is not itself. This creates 'lines of flight'; from life itself we imagine all the becomings of life, using the human power of imagination to overcome the human" (Colebrook, 2001: 129). Planetary ethics reminds us our intersubjectivity, biohistorical agency, and political ontology of becoming.

Pedagogy of the Planetary Ethics: Listening to a Dalit Testimony; but not 'from the margins'; of course, it is form the de-margined margin!

In his autobiography—*Kandal kadukalkidayil ente jeevitham* [My Life in the midst of Mangrove Plants]—Kallel Pokudan, a Dalit activist, argues for an eco-political agency. His eco-political agency is explained in the book autobiographically. He explains how he has become an eco-political activist. Kallel Pokkudan says it was his search for a de-casteist identity that led to him to a planetary agency. He had three specific options before him to reject his caste identity: one was to embrace communism and to become a *pulaya*-communist. Later he came to the understanding that the Communist party can never understand the life of a Dalit. The second option was to embrace Christianity and to become a *pulaya*-Christian. Accepting the fact that a *pulayan* can never be an integral part of the Church in Kerala, he rejected that possibility. The third option was to become an activist for his *pulaya*-community. But, he realized that at that time the *pulaya* community was not capable enough to accommodate a self reflexive-communist activist. He writes: "For a long time I didn't do anything. Then I slowly started to preserve the kandal [mangrove plants] nearby my house. It is how I became Kandal Pokudan" (Pokudan, 2000: 10). Kandal Pokudan is not just a name; rather it is his life, politics, and becoming/belonging himself—of course a political ontology of planetarity. Whitney Bauman is extremely right when he says; "Planetarity opens up to different ways of becoming human and possibly posthuman" (Bauman, 2014: 152).

Post-Script

The focus of this paper has been to propose a method for contemporary Christian ethics in India. Christian ethics in India has to recognize the contemporary epistemological context of multi-disciplinarity. Christian ethics in India has to overcome the problem of God and the other as it is inherited from the Western enlightenment metaphysics and ontology. Christian ethics in India must look into the contemporary theological/philosophical/theoretical resources in order to develop a radical political ontology and a materialist theology. Planetary ethics, as it proposes the pedagogy of listening to the silenced, provides a radical method of doing Christian ethics in India today. The role of theological academia, the Church, and the theologian is to formulate the Biblical hermeneutics, liturgical discourses, and ministerial models that enable them to listen to the voices of the silenced which is im/possible for them unless they re-articulate their own ontology.

References

Aruna Gnanadason, "Feminist Ethics: A Search for Meaning and Hope from the Margins," in *Ethical Issues in the Struggles for Justice*, ed. Daniel Chetti and M. P. Joseph (Tiruvalla: CSS/BTTBPSA, 1998).

Claire Colebrook, *Gilles Deleuze* (New York and London: Routledge, 2001).

David Tracy, *On Naming the Present: God, Hermeneutics, and Church* (Maryknoll, New York: Orbis Books, 1994).

Eduardo Mendieta, ed., *Beyond Philosophy: Ethics, History, Marxism, and Liberation Theology* (Oxford, UK: Rowman & Littlefield Publishers, 2003).

Emmanuel Levinas, *Totality and Infinity: An Essay on Exteriority* (Pittsburgh, PA: Duquesne University Press, 1969).

Enrique Dussel, "The World–System': Europe as 'Center' and Its 'Periphery' beyond Eurocentrism," in *Beyond Philosophy: Ethics, History, Marxism, and Liberation Theology*, ed. Eduardo Mendieta (Oxford, UK: Rowman & Littlefield Publishers, 2003).

Gabrielle Hiltmann, "Introduction: Accounting for the Other: Towards an Ethics of Thinking," in *The Other: Feminist reflections in Ethics*," ed. Helen Fielding et al. (New York: Palgrave Macmillan, 2007).

Gayatri Chakravorty Spivak, *A Critique of Postcolonial reason: Toward a History of the Vanishing Present* (Cambridge: Harvard University Press, 1999).

George Zachariah, *Alternatives Unincorporated: Earth Ethics from the Grassroots* (London: Equinox, 2011).

Homi K Bhabha, *The location of Culture* (London and New York: Routledge, 1994).

Jane Bennett, *Vibrant Matter: a political ecology of things* (Durham and London: Duke University Press, 2010).

Jea Sophia Oh, *A Postcolonial Theology of Life: Planetarity East and West* (California: Sopher Press, 2011).

Judith Butler, *Parting Ways: Jewishness and the Critique of Zionism* (New York: Columbia University Press, 2012).

J Russell Chandran, *Christian Ethics* (Delhi: ISPCK, 2004).

Kallel Pokudan, *Kandal Kadukalkidayil ente jeevitham* (Paghayangadi: Media Magic, 2000).

K. C. Abraham, *Transforming Vision: Theological-Methodological Paradigm Shifts* (Tiruvalla: CSS, 2006).

Mayra Rivera, *The Touch of Transcendence: A Postcolonial Theology of God* (Louisville, London: Westminster John Knox Press, 2007).

Michel R. Ott, 'The Notion of the Totality: "Other" and its Consequence in the Critical Theory of Religion and the Rational Choice Theory of Religion' in *Marx, Critical Theory, and Religion, A Critique of Rational Choice* edited by warren S. Goldstein (Boston: Brill, 2006), 143.

M. Stephen, *Introducing Christian Ethics* (Delhi: ISPCK, 2013);

Peniel Jesudasan Rufus Rajkumar, "The Diversity and Dialectics of Dalit Dissent and Implications for a Dalit Theology of Liberation," in *Dalit Theology in the Twenty-first Century*, eds., Sathianathan Clarke et al. (New Delhi: Oxford, 2010).

Ritu Birla, "Postcolonial Studies" in *Can the Subaltern Speak? Reflections on the History of an Idea*, Morris RC ed., (New York: Colubia Press, 2010).

Sara Ahmed, *Strange Encounters: Embodied Others in Post-Coloniality* (London and New York: Routledge, 2000), 142.

Somen Das, *Christian Ethics and Indian Ethos* (Delhi: ISPCK, 2009).

Spivak, *Planetary Love: Spivak, Postcoloniality and Theology*, eds. Moore S.D and Mayra Rivera (New York: Fordham University Press, 2011), 62.

Wati Longchar, *Returning to the Mother Earth* (Kolkata: PCTA, 2012).

Whitney A Bauman, *Religion and Ecology: developing a planetary ethic* (New York: Columbia University Press, 2014).

Y. T. Vinayaraj, *Intercessions: Theology, Liturgy, and Politics* (New Delhi: ISPCK, 2015).

Y. T. Vinayaraj, "Ecumenism and the Marginality," in *Prophetic Ecumenism*, ed. Christopher Raj Kumar (Tiruvalla: NCCI & CSS, 2014).

9

Re-claiming Contextual Theologies as Political Theologies: Transforming Theological Education in India*

Introduction

Celebrating 500 years of Reformation and 200 years of the formation of the Serampore College mark a significant moment in the life of the Indian Church and Indian theological academia. It is an important moment for the Indian Church to gratefully acknowledge and admire the lives and ministry of the great missionaries and visionaries who initiated the efforts to make Christian Theology indigenous and contextual. Of course, the last 200 years of theological pilgrimage in India has gone through various phases of transition and transformation, which really testify the fecundity and significance of theological academia in the public witness of the Church in India.

---

* Paper presented at the National Seminar organized by the Senate of Serampore College University on 31st July at CSI Synod secretariat, Chennai.

The initial task was to formulate Indian Christian Theology in dialogue with the Hindu philosophical/religious traditions and this has been continued till the emergence of the ecumenical theologies of inter-religious dialogue in the post-independent period in India. the Eruption of the Latin American Liberation Theology and Black Theology in 1970s/80s marked a new era in the whole Third World theology and it impacted heavily the Indian theological academia with the formation of the contextual theological imaginations.

The formation of contextual theologies in India marks a significant turning point in Indian Christian Theology in terms of its methodology and content. It was a radical shift from the philosophical discourses to the ethos and the pathos of the struggling masses in India. Indian Christian theology was invoked and provoked to get baptized in the cry of the marginalized. As the authors of the book titled *Dalit Theology in the Twenty-First Century: Discordant Voices, Discerning Pathways*, Sathianathan Clarke, Deenabandhu Manchala and Philip Vinod Peacock write in the introduction, 'the contextualization of Christian theology in India in terms of Dalit imaginations makes theology incarnated into the flesh and blood of the broken bodies in India (Clarke, et al., 2011: 9). K. C Abraham, the pioneering Indian Christian theologian, offered a systematic framework for contextual theologies in India: (1) the experiences of the marginalized as the context of theology; (2) counter knowledges as theological resources; (3) contextual theologies as liberative praxis (Abraham, 1993: 15-22). The unrelenting commitment of the Indian theological academia to strengthen the contextual theological imaginations in India has resulted in the transformation of the excluded communities in India, and hence it is to be acknowledged and appreciated in the very occasion of the bi-centenary celebration of Indian theological academia.

However, it is time to review the content and the method of contextual theologies in India in order to re-signify Indian Christian Theology in the contemporary context. The contemporary context is fluid, contestatory and complex. The Neo-liberal economy and its project of destitution (otherwise called empire by Hardt & Negri) have created a virtual world of homogeneity and universality where there is no clear distinction in terms of space, gender, and culture.

Gilles Deleuze calls this 'territorialization' and 'de-territorialization' (Antonio Negri & Michael Hardt, 2004: xiii). In this juncture, the question before us is that, is there any relevance for a contextual theology in a virtual world of interaction, interchange, and exchange? How do we define context in a context where the fixity of the context is being questioned? Do the contextual theologies need a methodological change in the post-liberation theology context where the liberation theology is interrogated for its Euro-centric epistemic foundations? Have the contextual theologies in India become inadequate to revitalize the Church to respond to the political concerns of the marginalized in the post-globalized era? Then what would be the epistemological foundations of re-claiming contextual theologies as political theologies in India today? Taking Dalit theology as a case, this paper tries to offer a constructive proposal for a methodological shift in Indian Christian Theology and thereby re-locates contextual theologies as political theologies in India.

Textuality of the Con-text: Re-locating Context in Contextual Theologies

Contextual theologies have envisioned a praxiological methodology that made the incarnation of Christian theology possible in India. This incarnation was methodologically rendered as Inculturation and Contextualization. One of the most important issues that the postcolonialists point out is that the Inculturation/Contextualization was a missionary 'gaze' from above up on the 'indigenous other', who is waiting to be humanized. It was an empowering 'gaze' to the people from below. As Felix Wilfred rightly points out, at the heart of this Inculturation process, there is a colonial notion of the pre-existent Universal Church (Felix Wilfred, 2018: 19). Of course, whether the postcolonialists agree or not, the impact of this 'colonial gaze' was productive and transformative at least for the lives of the endogenous people in India. They were able to re-locate their social position and social agency in the crucial context of casteism and the political marginalization. The problem is that this 'colonial gaze' upon the 'indigenous people' is still maintained in theological methodology and the 'indigenous people' are still at the position of marginality waiting to be humanized and transformed (Sugirtharajah: 2008). This problem exists due to the essentialization of the 'indigenous identity' and social position of the people from 'below.'

Theorizing the subaltern, Gayatri Chakravorty Spivak problematizes the fixity of identities and offers a rhetorical position of de-othering the other. In Spivakian epistemology, the subaltern (the subordinated other) is not a fixed position of the other; rather, it is a contested position where the other deconstructs its otherness and re-locates itself as political subject of transformation. The Spivakian 'other' hesitates to be an 'other' so that she can never be fixed as the other-the binary opposite of the 'Self.' The Spivakian 'other' escapes the hegemonic process of otherization, through which the 'Self' maintains its dominance on the 'other.' The 'other' in Spivakian epistemology exercises its embodied potentiality (auto immunity) to overcome the programme of otherization.

Alluding to Jacques Derrida, Spivak challenges the fixity of the context and allows it to be something other than this by deconstructing the history of its constitution. That means, the Dalit context is not a fixed context waiting to be transformed by the 'colonial (empowering) gaze' from outside. It is not an essential position; so that anyone can easily locate it as a 'site of compassion' and 'identification.' Dalit con-text, in 'other' wise, is a creative and potential site within it and has the capacity to deconstruct it by offering new discourses and practices of both resistances and reconfigurations. Dalit pathos is not just the 'essentialized site of victimization;' rather it is the potential site of resources that make Dalits social agents and political subjects in the post-globalized era. Dalit identity or Dalit context is to be re-located in a deconstructive/de-othered rhetorical position through which Dalits deny its fixed position of the other, the subaltern, and the margin. When we celebrate the marginality of the margin, we legitimize otherwise, the centrality of the center.

What is being argued here is that the Dalit context in Contextual Theologies is not essentialized, fixed and static but fluid, enigmatic and alluric which needs to be approached with caution. It is not a 'loose' place (*terra nullis*—a barren place which is waiting to be colonized) so that everyone can come and offer their solidarity and the love for the other. It is a political place of transformation that demands the deconstruction of the self and the other, the center and the margin, elite and the subaltern. Dalit context as the site of new epiphanies rather than the site of fixed identities demands a paradigm shift in contextual theological methodology. The task of Dalit theology is to make this political process of becoming of Dalit bodies visible and to invoke the other life-worlds to see, feel and share this transformative political practice of being and belonging in the contemporary epistemological context. Here, Dalit Theology as the contextual theology becomes a political theology as it opens up its 'imagined boundary' for the mutual engagement, interrogation and sublimation of all.

Trans-disciplinarity of Theology: The Multifariousness of Contextual Theologies

Christian theology as a discipline emerged in the historical encounter with philosophy and modern science. Knowledge that is considered as the absolute and fixed was the modern Western Enlightenment logic and thus it paved the way for Euro-centrism and colonialism. Thus any knowledge, that claims infallibility and totality within it, is hegemonic and exclusive. This can happen even to contextual theologies. If the boundary of the contextual theologies is closed then there is no life existing within. Life remains in a biologically conducive ecosystem where the imagined boundaries of the ecosystems are organically connected and linked with. Whether it is theology, ideology, science, religion, gender or culture, the closed boundaries invite fundamentalism, totalitarianism, and finally death. The methodological exclusivism that has been offered to Dalit theology by Arvind P. Nirmal was in fact to block the political and epistemological hijacking of an indigenous theology especially in its 'childhood' period. But, it should not be used as a methodological strategy to fix the boundary of Dalit Theology forever. Neither Dalit theology nor Dalit life-world is a closed 'regime of truth' by which it claims a complacent territory and culture. Dalit identity politics sometimes in history has been misused to claim the exclusive and clogged nature of Dalit knowledges and practices.

Caste as a social knowledge and practice demands a collective interrogation of both Dalits and non-Dalits. Caste does not exclusively remain within the Dalit-life world or the elite-life world which have already been re-territorialized and de-territorialized in the contemporary context of Neo-capitalism. At the same time caste has taken new forms and shapes today, which cannot be addressed by the old solutions of anti-casteism. Anti-casteism, as it is offered by the modern neo-liberal dreams, is deceptive and fake and hence Dalit theology has to find out new ways of economic justice and freedom. Ambedkar envisaged a method of multifarious engagements to challenge caste in the colonial modernity and envision a reformed political subjectivity for the former untouchables. Methodologically, he engaged with Buddhism, Marxism and Western Pragmatism to re-imagine the social position of Dalits in modern India. Ambedkar was convinced of the need of the 'strategical' engagement with the colonial governance, missionary education and Indian nation-state to elevate the social position of a historically down-trodden people.

The question of inter-disciplinarity comes in when we address the concerns the new formations of caste practices in India today. It is in the political process of re-imagining new social democracy and common practices of fraternity, justice and equality, caste is denied and nullified epistemologically and politically. Thus, the task of Dalit theology is to engage with all other de-casteist knowledges and practices and to respond to them theologically and Biblically. It is to see, participate and feel the fragments of de-casteism in other religious traditions, Scriptures, political ideologies, cultural art and music, which re-shape Dalit Theology polydoxical in content (Catherine Keller & Laurel C. Schneider, 2011). If Dalit theology continues to remain in the (Western) Christian hermeneutical world, it is going to be irrelevant and impotent in the contemporary Indian context of Neo-liberal Economy and culture. Only by transcending the (Western) Christian hermeneutical world and engaging with its cultural/philosophical others such as secularism, materialism and atheism, Dalit theology can become a radical de-casteist political practice in India. Jayakiran Sebastian has raised this methodological issue of trans-disciplinarity of Dalit theology long before (Sebastian, 2008: 84):

> Dalit theology, which at one stage was accused of being a narrow theological 'ism', of relevance only to those who had the 'pathos' experience, or were in empathetic or sympathetic agreement with it, draws its strength from the rich and complex inter-connections with the methodological possibilities thrown up by epistemological inquiry in the spectrum of fields of knowledge. In other words, the strength of Dalit theology lies precisely in the possibility of its inter-disciplinarity, something that needs to be acknowledged and fostered.

Interrogating the 'Ethos of Transcendence': De-stabilizing the Foundations of Contextual Theologies

Mark Lewis Taylor interrogates Christian theology for grounding its epistemology in the 'ethos of transcendence' that helps Christian theology to be insensitive to the agonistic politics of the tortured bodies in the world (Taylor, 2011: xi). For him, the God of the (Western) Christian theology is the transcendent God—the Wholly Other—God who offers his salvation to the world from outside. The 'ethos of transcendence', as it legitimizes a point of salvation outside or beyond the 'weight of the world', or 'the agonistic politics of the tortured bodies in the world' makes Church/theological academia comfortable in keeping public witness (diakonia) distinctive from its being (ontology). Taylor expounds that Christian theology is still remaining in the dichotomy between being and doing, secular and sacred, God and the world, matter and spirit, theism and atheism and this problem of dichotomy is solved by the notion of the economy of salvation, through which the salvation is offered to the world by the grace of God while maintaining the ontological distinction between God and the world. In short, Christian theology's God is a transcendent God who is ontologically unrelated to the world/matter/body while offering it salvation through grace. Nirmal, on the other hand, looked for a 'de-transcendent God' or an 'enmattered God' who ontologically relates to the world/matter/body and thereby offered a materialist epistemology for Dalit theology based on Lokayata philosophy (Nirmal, 1991: 106).

For Nirmal, to challenge the Vedic-transcendent philosophies of God and Maya, it is inescapable for Dalit theology to locate itself in the materialist Indian philosophy (Lokayata). What is so unfortunate that, after Nirmal, no Dalit theologian followed this pathway and continued this search. And on the other hand, Dalit theologians borrowed the doctrine of God from the (Western) Christian Theology and offered salvation to Dalit bodies through sacraments. Ambedkar was convinced enough about this inadequacy of Christian theology and opted for Buddhism where we don't see even a transcendent legitimizing point—God or Soul. Following the Indian materialist philosophical tradition, Ambedkar believed in the political process of being/becoming/belonging in the democratic community through which Dalits envision a new political subjectivity. In fact, Ambedkar was offering a political philosophy/theology of an enmattered God/embodied God/immanent God where both the theist and atheist notions are engaged with and challenged. In the same vein of thought, the post-Western philosopher and theologian Giorgio Agamben defines his doctrine of God who is 'profane' in content (Agamben: 2008).

What is argued here is that Indian contextual theologies are in need of an imminent turn. It is a radical turn to re-locate Indian contextual theologies in the epistemic foundations of local and indigenous materialist traditions and thereby become political in content. The turn to immanence, as it was argued by Gilles Deleuze, will help the contextual theologies to overcome the issue of dichotomy between world and God, body and Spirit, secular and sacred, theism and atheism, spirituality and materiality and thereby envision a post-Western/post-colonial/de-contextualized Christian theology based on Indian epistemological resources. Achille Mbembe, the African philosopher and thinker alludes to the salvific content of the crucified body of Jesus Christ in which he finds rich resources for a political philosophy in the postcolonial world.

> The body of the dead man on the cross is not reducible on its fundamental thingness. In fact, the figurative dimension is already there, clothed in appearance: the face of the shadow (Mbembe, 2001: 213).

Conclusion

Re-claiming contextual theologies as political theologies in India today demands at least three turns: (1) the turn towards the deconstruction of con-texts; (2) the turn towards Polydoxy that ensures multifarious engagements and trans-disciplinary practices; and (3) the turn towards immanence through which the dichotomy between God and the world, Church and Mission is destabilized. Contextual theologies are to be envisaged as political theologies in India today and thereby provoke the Indian Church to really participate in the political process of justice, rather than offering salvation to the world through its transcendent theologies and liturgies. Let the bi-centenary discussions help us to envision new transitions and transformations in theological academia and Church!

References

Achille Mbembe, *On the Postcolony* (New York: California University Press, 2001).

Arvind, P. Nirmal, *Heuristic Explorations* (Madras: GLTC, 1990).

Catherine Keller and Lauren C. Schneider, *Polydoxy: Theology of Multiplicity and Relations* (London: Rutledge, 2011).

Felix Wilfred, "Asian Christianities and Theologies through the Lens of Postcolonialism," in *Concilium* 2018/1 London, pp. 15-26.

Gayatri Chakravorty Spivak, *Other Asias* (Oxford: Blackwell, 2008).

Giorgio Agamben, *The Church and the Kingdom* (London and Calcutta: Seagull Books, 2012).

Gilles Deleuze, *Difference and Repetition*, trans. P. Patton (London: Continum, 2004).

James Massy, ed., *Contextual Theological Education* (Delhi: ISPCK, 1993).

Jayakiran Sebastian, 'Can We Now Bypass that truth,' *Transformations* 2.5 & 3 April & July 2008.

Mark Lewis Taylor, *The Theological and The Political* (Minneapolis: Fortress Press, 2011).

Michel Hardt and Antonio Negri, *The Empire* (New York: Penguin Press, 2004).

Michel Hardt and Antonio Negri, *Multitude: War and Democracy in the Age of Empire* (New York: Penguin Press, 2004).

Sathianathan Clarke, et.al. eds., *Dalit Theology in the Twenty-First Century: Discordant Voices, Discerning Pathway* (London: Oxford University Press, 2010).

Sugirtharajah., ed., *Still at the Margins* (London: T&T Clark, 2008).

10

Cross as the Fulcrum of Politics: M. M. Thomas with Vattimo and Agamben*

Introduction

The relationship between theology and politics is always complex and contestatory. Has theology ever been apolitical? Or has politics ever been atheological? Are they distinct, interchangeable, alternative, parallel, polar, complimentary or supplementary? Political thinkers have already exposed the integral connection between political thinking and the history of the West and hence with Christendom. Giorgio Agamben, the well-known Italian political thinker emphatically exposes the mysterious relationship between theology and politics in Western tradition. John D. Caputo and Catherine Keller underline this thought and thus said: "any renewal of political order requires a renewal of theology" in Western tradition. Taking a cue from the political theologian Carl Schmitt, Agamben argues that

* Talk offered at Dr. M. M. Thomas Birth centenary National Colloquium, 26-28th January 2016 at JMM study centre, Trivandrum.

in Western tradition, understandings of political sovereignty correlate with the understanding of divine sovereignty. This is well-evident in the Hobbesian political theory of modern state, democracy, and politics, which is founded on the notion of the sovereign God. What he is trying to explicate here is that Christian theology has always been political in content in Western tradition.

The contemporary political thought, on the other hand, envisions a post-secular and post-religion epistemological context. Post-religion signifies Christianity after Christendom and God after the death of God. In this new context, Christianity is invoked and provoked to be deconstructed and to be in dialogical existence with other religions. God in this context is a weak God as we see in the life of Jesus Christ on the cross. Cross, as it poses itself as the political space of crucifixion and resurrection, becomes a sign and symbol of the contemporary political theology, unlike the atonement theories in antiquity by which the cross has been interpreted as the site of divine sacrifice and love towards humankind who had gone astray from the divine. It had been theologized as a benevolent act of a sovereign God who graciously incarnates/intervenes into the human predicament of sin. On the contrary, the contemporary political philosophers like, Gianni Vattimo, Giorgio Agamben, Gilles Deleuze, Alain Badiou, and Judith Butler engages with the theology of cross in order to substantiate a radical political practice in the post-secular/post-religion context.

M. M. Thomas was one of the post-independent Indian Christian theologians who found significance in the theology of the crucified God to expose the failure of the Absolutist political power of the state in India. Thomas' theology, in the process of formulating a radical political theology in India, offered a political logic of forgiveness founded on his theology of the crucified God. It was an exhortation to the secular state to imagine its post-secular identity and to the religions to think about a secular Koinonia. However, the inadequacy to address the postcolonial aspects of post-independent Indian politics and their implications on contemporary theology necessitate a re-reading or critical engagement with his theological imaginations. This paper tries to re-read Thomas' understanding of state, democracy, and politics by highlighting his theology of the crucified God in dialogue with the postmodern political thinkers—Gianni Vattimo and Giorgio Agamben. The list of postmodern/postcolonial thinkers who make use of the Biblical resources to formulate their political theories is very vast. The selection of Vattimo and Agamben is based on their close affinity with the Christian theological heritage and their critique of the dogmatic Christian faith from within. Despite the epistemological divergences between the postmodern/postcolonial political thinkers and M. M. Thomas, it is interesting to see some of the converging points in the theology of cross especially in terms of their consensus to formulate a materialist foundation for Christian theology.

Crucified God: Taking Stock of Contemporary Political Thought

i. Weak Ontology: Gianni Vattimo

Gianni Vattimo is a prominent social democratic politician and a distinguished Italian philosopher. Postmodernism, according to Vattimo, is an epoch of transformation of ontology (the notion of being). Modernity developed the notion—"forgetting of being." For modernity, the constitution of being is an innocent activity—nothing official about it—because it is the European, white, male being which is at the center of all discourses of politics, philosophy, and theology. Postmodernity dismantles this certainty of modern ontology and metaphysics and opens up a new sphere of multiple interpretations of being. Following the Nietzsche's "death of God theology" and Heideggerian "ontology of Dasein," Vattimo offers a political theory of 'weak ontology' which means that the meaning of being is embodied in manifold interpretations (Vattimo, 2003: 91-92). Vattimo finds the theological foundation of this 'weak ontology' in the theology of cross where the sovereignty of God is denied and the violence of the modern metaphysics is rejected.

According to Vattimo, "the weak ontology" or "the ontology of the weakening of (the western) Being" supplies philosophical reasons for preferring a liberal, tolerant, and democratic society to an authoritarian and totalitarian one. It stands for the emancipatory politics as it attends to the cry of the victims in this world. It signifies a post-metaphysical epoch where the identities are understood in terms of our relationality, mutuality and multiplicity. The (Western) logic of development at the cost of the non-Western communities and cultures are to be revoked on the basis of this 'weak ontology' and metaphysics. The capitalist logic of economy has to be revoked in order to understand the struggles of the marginalized people in the colonized worlds. On the whole, 'the weak ontology' signifies a post-Western/colonial philosophy, science, economics, culture, and politics.

Alluding to Rene Girard, Vattimo argues that natural religions are founded upon the need to create victims to keep order in society. There is a metaphysics that connects sacred with violence. A sacrificial scapegoat is killed to prevent the society's destruction. The Bible reveals this victim-based mechanism. For Vattimo, Jesus was not sacrificing himself for his Father; rather he was trying to expose this victim-based mechanism. The Cross, by exposing the violence connected to the sacred, becomes an act of emancipation (Vattimo, 2003: 109). Jesus on the cross abolishes the nexus between violence and the sacred. Cross exemplifies the divine act of kenosis. Kenosis is the message of the weakening of God. Imitating God is listening to the message of weakening as principle. It is this message that enables us to weaken the sovereign political structures that create victims. For Vattimo, faith in Christ is nothing but a faith in the weakening of strong structures (metaphysical, political, and religious) that restricted multiple interpretations of ontology. Weakening or nihilism, for Vattimo, is not a negative/pessimistic location; rather it is the 'sole opportunity' for emancipation from the violence of metaphysics. Vattimo, by rejecting the metaphysical foundation of the act of politics, argues for a political ontology of actuality that finds meaning in all local argumentative political practice (Vattimo, 2003: 88).

ii. Ontology of Inoperativity: Giorgio Agamben

Giorgio Agamben is the professor of philosophy and Aesthetics at the University of Verona in Italy. Agamben's political thought begins with his distinction between political life (*bios*) and bare life (*zoe*) or non-political life. For Agamben, as citizens of the state, we become juridical subjects. We all are born to a political system and thereby we are denied of our bare life—life we have simply as human beings. Thus the stateless—the slaves, the unborn, the refugees, the inhabitants of the camps are non-humans. Here Agamben reveals his thesis that the marginality of those people are legally legitimized and sanctioned within. The notion of the sovereign state legitimizes this 'state of exception'—the state of 'excluded in' and 'included out' (Agamben, 1998: 11).

Re-reading the Pauline theology of cross, Agamben argues that crucifixion is the point of revocation of our subjectivity. Christian vocation is a call (*kletos*) to revoke all our vocations. All other vocations such as slave/master; woman/man; Jew/Gentile, etc. are constituted juridically. Call to be part of *ekklesia* is to crucify the juridical subjectivity and to reconstitute new subjectivity in Jesus Christ. The vocation's revocation involves death—crucifixion. The resurrection is the revocation of the vocation on behalf of the Church—'the coming community' and thereby becomes the Christian political agent. Agamben argues that the revoked and crucified vocation of the Christian political agent should be evident in their 'quietist political action.' The Pauline usage of the Greek word *katargeo* which means deactivation or de-energizing or emptying out, connected to the concept of crucifixion, explains the quietest political action of the Christian agent. It is nothing but the act of inoperativity of the juridical subjectivity and to become part of a collective subjectivity—'the coming community.' To be a new creation in Christ is not exactly or simply to take a new identity; it is to empty one's already-in-place identity of juridical significance without thereby removing it (Griffiths, 2013: 167-197). Christian political agent, a citizen with vocation revoked, is a member of the remnant who acts in the Kairos of the messianic now. In Agamben's view the Christian agent is supposed to crucify her political interest and thereby do politics without law through quietism, skepticism, hope and lament.

The Messianic call is to deactivate the juridical subjectivity and thus become bare life-the life which is not bounded by the law. It is nothing but the sphere of the church—the body of the crucified Christ. Those who live in the *ekklesia* are in a sphere of weakness which alone makes possible the use of their emptied but still present vocations. The church, in this sense, is community without the law; it is what Agamben likes to call *the coming community*, the community that occupies *the time that remains*, the community which is outside of the law. It is the location of bare life—the crucified body of the victims of the world. Ecclesiology in Agamben's political thought is a political ontology which embodies a cruciform ontology. Agamben's political theory based on the cross does not make us inactive; rather it asks us to be ontologically different and actively participate in the contemporary political programme of reconfiguring the social positions and subjectivities. The Christian political agent is an active political advocate who sometimes becomes the activist (barricades, protests, martyrdoms) or verbal (broadsheets, blogs, street-corner speeches), and may be within ordinary legal bounds (voting, running for office) or goes in excess (civil disobedience, revolution).

Crucified God: Political Theology of M. M. Thomas

M. M. Thomas' political thought is founded in the interstice between ideology and faith. Prophetic faith, according to Thomas, is "the spiritual opening of our hearts to the cries of the victims in response to the passion of God. Political theology translates it in terms of understanding the situation of the victims and formulating the ends and means to be pursued to effect a transformation of the situation. In that way faith needs ideology in the struggle for justice" (Thomas, 1996: 113). Though his teleological anthropology and its dialectical materialist relationship it positions him in the Hegelian/Marxist epistemological framework, Thomas overcomes its inherent limitation by opening the Hegelian closed ontology with the Christian faith that keeps the internal potentiality of human bodies and social bodies vibrantly. Church, as the body of the crucified God, for Thomas, is the embodiment of this potentiality and vibrancy as it reconstitutes its ontology in solidarity with the victims of this world.

Responding to the declaration of Emergency in 1975, Dr. Thomas interrogated the totalitarianism and the authoritarianism of the sovereign state in India. Thomas wrote: "The price we pay for the peace of a police raj is that it will put large sections of the people, just beginning to awaken to their rights in the emerging society, back to sleep....Without some revolts and conflicts resulting from people's efforts to throw of their slavery and exploitative structures, poverty will remain with us forever. It is these revolts which have now been halted" (Thomas, 2000: 17). For Thomas, the state is a protector of human rights and it legitimizes peoples' desire for emancipation. His distinction between "conquering kingship" and "suffering servant hood" is very much helpful to understand his theology of state.

Thomas' theology of state is founded on his theology of cross. According to Thomas, the cross is the self-manifestation of the self-forgetting and self-sacrificing God. This crucified God in Jesus was giving a new direction to the Davidic kingdom which is established on sovereign power. The Crucified one is the negation of the totalitarian exercise of power over humans. The state is to serve the people, not to rule over the people. Thomas cites St. Matthew to clarify his theology of state: "You know that the rulers of the Gentiles lord it over them, and their great men exercise authority over them. It shall not be so among you; (...)but who ever would be first among you must be your slave; even as the Son of Man come not to be served but to serve; and to give his life as a ransom for many" (Mt. 20: 25-28). Thomas comments that the throne of David has been replaced by the kingdom community through the crucified and risen Jesus Christ (Thomas, 2006: 41).

Thomas argues that on the cross, Jesus Christ disarmed the rulers and the authorities of the world. The empire is defeated and nullified. Cross signifies the end of the totalitarian power and the beginning of a new community—kingdom community—a universal community where there are no dichotomies. In the new community, "there is no longer any distinction between Gentiles and Jews, circumcised and uncircumcised, barbarians, savages, slaves, and free me" (Col. 3:11). The new human community is constituted as a single body—the body of the crucified God in history. The crucified body of God is not a new thing; rather it is the body of the slain Lamb from the creation of the world and it continues to be slain till the end of the world fighting against the totalitarian forces of powers. The mark of crucifixion continues to be the sign of the suffering struggle of God against the principalities and powers till the end of the world. The mission of the Church today is to embody this mark of crucifixion and to reconstitute its ontology in solidarity with the victims of the world.

According to Thomas, the Church is entrusted with a prophetic diakonia to discharge its duty based on the servant-hood exemplified by the crucified God. Thomas writes: "The Church in India is called to proclaim the gospel of the crucified and risen Christ as the source of redemption of all spirituallties underlying religion as well as ideologies, and to demonstrate the Koinonia in Christ around the Eucharist as the nucleus of a movement of the larger Koinonia in Christ uniting peoples of diverse religions, ideologies and cultures—as well as the cosmos–with its bio-diversity" (Thomas, 1995: 82). Based on his theology of the cross, M. M. Thomas explains the features of the mission of the church in India: (1) the calling of the Church is to resist the idolatry of power and wealth and other gods of death in India's collective life, (2) to be in solidarity with the poor and the oppressed in their struggle for justice, and (3) the mission of the Church is to give up communal self-interest and self-identity for the sake of creating in India a secular national community in the midst of India's religious and ideological pluralism through manifesting a fellowship in Christ, transcending class, caste, ethnic and religious communal divisions (Thomas, 1990: 11).

However, what is lacking in the political theology of M. M. Thomas is that he was not attentive to the metamorphosis happening to the sovereign state as it was becoming the empire. In the context of empire, democracy assumes the global stature and national citizens become trans-national subjects which demand new analytical tools to assess the metamorphosis happening to post-globalized state and democracy. The empire assumes new cultural-religious-economic logic and manifestations that legitimize a multifaceted sovereign political power which has no single point of performance. The biopolitics of the empire assumes multiple origins and micro-formations. Here political becomes cultural and social and their ramifications in the micro-spaces of common living are even extended to human bodies. According to Antonio Negri, politics is the not the reaction-response of people against the state, rather, human life itself is political. Alluding to the Spinozian tradition, Negri makes us to think about a human body and social body which is prior to the biopolitical impact of the state on human life. In the Spinozian tradition, life has its own inherent potentiality to challenge the hegemonic practices and that politics of 'bare-life' is to be upheld for a radical political engagement. Negri calls it the politics of multitude. The political theory of multitude signifies a social living of 'common' which is capable enough to take on the global form of empire in its multiplicity and universality.

Conclusion

Denying the notion of the Sovereign God—the unitary foundation of our politics, philosophy, and theology, the contemporary political theology signifies the theology of multitude. The political theology of multitude signifies the God of multiplicity, alterity and fluidity based on the theology of the crucified God. Ontology is given the possibility to have multiple interpretations. According to the theology of multitude, life is embedded with divine potentiality and it is always endowed with bio-power to transform itself. The crucified body of Christ does not demand a transcendental God who comes from beyond to offer his gracious act of salvation, rather; it is in the agonies of the tortured bodies we find a tortured God. Here, God is not a transcendent omnipotent reality, rather; it is the inherent potentiality of life to deny the biopolitics of empire even in its micro-spaces of both human and social body. Contemporary political theology, differentiating itself from the medieval atonement theories and even from the modern political theologies locates itself in a social logic of salvation embodied in the cruciform existence of the countless victims in the world. Hence, it becomes a theology of embodiment and materialism. Political theology in India today signifies the theology of multitude; of course even going beyond the theology of M. M. Thomas in order to find meaning in the micro-politics of human life which is not at all obliged to have a teleological point of convergence such as class struggle or any other unilateral struggle against the state; rather promotes an ontology of actuality and multiplicity to find life in "common" in the context of empire.

References

Gianni Vattimo, *Nihilism & Emancipation: Ethics, Politics and Law* (New York: Columbia University Press, 2003).

Giorgio Agamben, *Homo Sacer: Sovereign Power and Bare Life*, Tran. Daniel Heller-Roazen Stanford: Stanford University Press, 1998).

M. M. Thomas, "The Church in India—Witness to the Meaning of the Cross Today," in *Future of the Church in India*, ed., Aruna Gnanadason (Nagpur: NCCI, 1990).

M. M. Thomas, *A Diaconal Approach to Indian Ecclesiology* (Rome & Tiruvalla: CIIS & CSS, 1995).

M. M. Thomas, *Responses to Tyranny* (Tiruvalla: CSS, 2000).

M. M. Thomas, *The Throne of David* (Tiruvalla: CSS, 2006).

Paul J. Griffiths, "The Cross as the Fulcrum of Politics: Exploring Agamben on Paul," in *Paul and the Philosophers,* edited by Ward Blanton and Hent de Vries (New York: Fordham University Press, 2013).

11

Daring to Walk: Challenges in Today's Fundamentalist, Religious and Political Arenas*

Introduction

The theme selected for our discussion is so crucial as it necessitates a serious deliberation on the socio-political and religious situation in India today. Fundamentalism whether it is religious or cultural has turned our social and political life problematic and deteriorating. The word fundamentalism signifies the notion of rigidity and fixity of beliefs and ideologies. It is a closed nature of truth where the possibility of interaction and dialogue is denied. When one religion or culture becomes fundamentalist, then it absolutizes itself over against the other and at the same time it denies the very existence of the other. The other is always problematic for a fundamentalist. The

* Key-note address offered at the Round Table Conference of UELCI on 6th February 2019 at Vishakapatanam.

Hindutva politics is the typical contemporary example in India where we see this absolutization of religiosity and politics. The violence and violations that this fundamentalist insurgence evokes are many and we read and experience them every day.

The following words of Vasram Sarvaiya, 23, one of the four Dalits who were beaten up on July 11, 2016, by *gau rakshakas* (cow protectors) in Gujarat, exemplify the intensity of the torture that the Dalits in India experience today as the immediate impact of cultural nationalism.

> My father was begging them to stop. He kept saying we had gone to pick up a dead cow, but they insisted we had killed it. They made us take off our shirts, tied us to a vehicle and used big lathis to hit us. More than 50 people were watching us get beaten, including some policemen, but no one helped. Instead, they were filming it on mobile phones. We would never kill an animal. When it is dead they call us to remove the carcass. For centuries our community has done this work. Why are they suddenly talking about cow protection? (Anupama Katakam, 2016: 117).

The country is slowly getting saffronized and all the pillars of democracy are being manipulated in favour of the fascist forces. The administrative, legislative, Judiciary and all other public and private enterprises are being manipulated. The net result is the erosion of secular and democratic values from our public life. The vigourous entry of the neo-capitalist forces and the reign of the market in alliance with the fascist forces, weaken the notion of the welfare-state and thus it has become an obedient servant to the global economic net-work of power, otherwise called the empire. What is interesting here is the illegitimate alliance between religion, politics and the economy. The legitimization of the 'suicide economy' (Vandana Shiva) and the subsequent process of the destitution of Indian farmers, the cultural otherization of the socially excluded communities, and the increasing violence against women and children mark the crucial contemporary Indian socio-political arena where the weak and the vulnerable become *bare-lives* (Giorgio Agamben).

Let me bring to your attention one recent example from my state-Kerala. Sabarimala is a known Hindu temple which has been opened for all irrespective of gender and caste for centuries. However, it was hijacked by the upper caste people and that managed to get a verdict from the Kerala High Court in 1990 denying the entry of women into the temple. Recently the honourable Supreme Court issued a new verdict to open it for all, including women. The Sangh Parivar forces initiated rampant violence and calamities against women who tried to enter into the temple, in the name of their impure status. This is a typical example of the illegitimate nexus between fundamentalist religious groups who never respect the values of democracy and Constitution and follow the gospel of the global empire. The political parties and the social groups that support this movement are the same groups that advocate for the program of reservation on the basis of economic status.

The question that matters for us is where the Indian Church is in this critical situation. We don't see any church raising its hands for justice to be done for the weak and the vulnerable. Some churches are in solidarity with the ruling political power. Some others are busy with their own internal problems within and without. The so-called established ecumenical movements have disappeared. They have become prophets on leave! It was a similar situation when the prophet Isaiah in the Old Testament called for an act of repentance and transformation from the side of the people of God by retreating to their original call and commission. If the Church neglects its role to be a just community in the context of violence, violation, and death, its call is being nullified and it becomes just an institution in the world. Thus DARING TO WALK in the midst of challenges is the only way out for the Church to reclaim its identity and existence.

Daring to Dream....

The Bible always invokes the Church to return to its original call and commission. It provokes the Church to dare to dream even in the midst of desperation and hopelessness. Particularly, the text Isaiah 11: 1-9 asks us to dream in the midst of crises and not just to walk. Exile, for the people of God, was not just time of persecution; rather it was a time of soliloquy. It was a time of radical imaginations.

Walter Brueggemann, the Old Testament scholar, invokes us to uphold radical imaginations even in the midst of Alien/nation, otherization, and marginalization. There are three radical visions that Isaiah wanted to instill in the life of the people of God in exile.

i. **Radical Vision of God**: God in the time of exile is the Messiah, the one who comes from within their own history. We see here a radical shift in the imagination of God. In chapter 6, we see a sovereign God who sits on the throne and receives all kinds of praise and worship. Here in this chapter we see a God of justice who is to come from within history. Redemption is not just a transcendent experience; rather it is to come from the re-imagination of our power relations.

   The challenge before the Church today is to participate in the process of making our social relationships just and fair and thereby to experience the God of justice in history. As Dr. M. M. Thomas clearly stated, when the Church lives for its own rights and benefits, it becomes a failed saint—an evil. The religiosity and the spirituality that the Church is expected to promote today is nothing but a *response-able spirituality* (Fr. Dr. Samuel Rayan) which stems from our integral engagement with the world. It is here that the Church is challenged to check whether it follows a response-able spirituality or other worldly-spirituality today. It is here, M. M. Thomas' call for the secular meaning of Christ becomes paradigmatic.

ii. **Radical Vision of Politics**: As per the vision of Isaiah, justice is foundational for social relationships. Social relationships are always political in content. Justice is nothing but to provide rights to the weak and to enable the vulnerable to lead a fair life in this world of discrimination and violence. It is to judge the people beyond the law of the state. It is 'outlaw justice' when the law of the state becomes ineffective and useless. The 'outlaw justice' is the justice of the Messiah. The 'undeadness of Jesus on the cross' exemplifies this 'outlaw justice' that resists the law of the empire and provides a fair life to the tortured and the agonized.

The Church is challenged today to practice a life of justice and to seek this Messianic time to come through its theological and liturgical life. Both theology and liturgy for a Messianic Church is political in content. Thus, political engagement is not at all an option for the Church to choose or not to choose but to live-out in this embodied *theopolitics* (John D. Caputo).

iii. **Radical Vision of Society**: According to Isaiah, the morality of social life is constituted in the re-imagination of power relationships. It is the radical concept of power that determines the morality of the society in favour of the poor and the weak. Isaiah envisages a pluriform democracy where one is oriented not to exercise its power over against the other but to respect the politics of difference of the other. It is a multifaceted–multilayered –polyphonic democracy where the 'irreducible singularity' of the other is respected and acknowledged in an ambience of mutuality and relationality. This is nothing but a radical vision of Messianic democracy where mutuality is affirmed and difference is acknowledged. Ambedkar calls this 'social democracy' where the excluded are included not as the 'charitable other' but as a social agency with power.

The Church is expected to envisage a polyphonic social democracy which is founded on equality, mutuality and freedom. Alluding to St. Paul, Dr. M. M. Thomas has spoken about the Church to be the sign and sacrament of the New Humanity in Christ, which is nothing but a multiple democracy. When Martin Luther identifies Eucharist as the Messianic practice of the Church to resist itself from becoming a captive in the Babylonian Empire, he envisages an open Church inclusive of all (Luther, 2001: 521).

Conclusion: Daring to Witness the Cross....

The Church daring to walk in the midst of challenges is provoked here to dare to dream—the dream of Messianic time and space in history. The hope of the Church is not located in the future; but in the 'now'—the immediacy of the messianic irruption. The Church is challenged here to be/come the church of the messianic irruption without any fear. It is in the struggles of the tortured masses through which they re-imagine themselves as the active agents of social democracy; the Church finds its ways to be/come the Church.

At the same time, there is always a 'cross-factor' in the public witness of the Church. The Church is the called-out community which is constituted for the world by denying itself for the cause. It is just a catalyst to be dissolved and vanished after its use. It is to be dissolved in the eruption of the historical hope of the crucified people in and around us. The institutionalized Church is a deviant church as it nullifies its constitutive principle within and without. It is provoked to feel the 'cross-factor' in and through the participation of struggles for a just and fair world around us.

Let me conclude this talk with the last words of Dr. Martin Luther King Jr. spoken just before his brutal assassination at Memphis in 1968:

> I choose to identify with the underprivileged. I choose to identify with the poor. I choose to give my life for the hungry. I choose to give my life for those who have been left out of the sunlight of opportunity. I choose to live for and with those who find themselves seeing life as a long and desolate corridor with no exit sign. This is the way I am going. If it means suffering a little bit, I am going that way. If it means sacrificing, I am going that way. If it means dying for them, I am going that way, because I heard a voice saying, "Do something for others (Sitkoff, 2008: 206).

We are called to dare to walk and to witness the cross in the midst of challenges till the end. What do these voices speak to us? "Let anyone who has an ear listen to what the Spirit is saying to the churches."

References

Anupama Katakam, "Torture and Backlash," *Frontline,* August 19, 2016, 117-121.

Harvard Sitkoff, *King: Pilgrimage to the Mountaintop* (New York: Hill and Wang, 2008).

Martin Luther, *The Babylonian Captivity of the Christian Church*, cited and analyzed by Alister E. McGrath, *Christian Theology: An Introduction* (UK: Blackwell Publishing: 2001), 521.

12

Ecumenical Formation and Theological Education in India*

Introduction

Ecumenism as the desire for the global unity of Christian communities and in wider sense, the integrity of whole Creation, is the foundational logic of theological education. In turn, theological education envisions the renewal of the churches and enriches its common witness in this world. Building up of a visionary leadership for the Church as well as the ecumenical movement is the task entrusted with the theological academy. In India, theological education had begun as the ecumenical project initiated by the Modern Missionary Movement and the Ecumenical Movement to build up a future generation of pastors and church leaders in India. However, the time has come to evaluate the fecundity of our current

* Talk offered at the Consultation on *Theological Formation and Capacity Building* organized by NCCI on 11th February, 2019 at HMI, Hyderabad.

theological education system as we celebrate bicentenary of the Serampore College.

There is a sharp criticism that our current theological education is losing its ecumenical character and thus become unecumenical in content and practice. On the other hand, ecumenism today has become a play of enclosures—enclosures in terms of ethnicity, caste/gender and denomination. Here, the spirit of ecumenism is loosened and a mechanical unity is formed while we retain our singularities. The marginal communities are the main losers here who have never been the custodians of either the Church's or the ecumenical resources. Enriching marginal communities to participate in the mission of the churches, which had been the focal point of ecumenical formation and theological education at the time of the beginning has now become a lost focus. In fact, it is in this crucial context, we initiate a discussion on the topic—Ecumenical Formation and the Theological Education in India.

In this paper, we discuss mainly two things: first, the challenges and prospects of the ecumenical formation in India. What do we mean by ecumenical formation? What are the prominent challenges that we face in India in the process of ecumenical formation? How does the Ecumenical Movement respond to those challenges today? These are some of the questions that we try to address in the first section. Secondly, we will try to understand the problems that we face in the program of theological education in India. Here we ask the question of why our theological education has become unecumenical and sectarian. What are the reasons behind the failures of the theological academy in promoting churches to do a fruitful common witness in India today? This paper is not intended to criticize the Ecumenical Movement and the theological program in India from the perspective of the marginalized and the excluded; rather it is intended to reclaim the integral link between theological education and the ecumenical formation, which has always been at the focus of enriching the marginal communities in the process of building up of a just community.

I. Ecumenical Formation in India: Challenges and Prospects

Having said the symbiotic relationship between ecumenical formation and theological education, let us discuss the meaning of becoming ecumenical in our own context. Becoming ecumenical in faith and witness as the foundational aspect of theological education challenges us today to come out of our closed ontologies and doctrinal fixities. Even our ecclesia-centric, ethnic-centric, and denomination-centric theological notions play a vital role in making ourselves unecumenical. Here, I would like to analyze the challenges and prospects of becoming ecumenical today through the life and witness of a great theologian from our country—M. M. Thomas whom I consider as a model ecumenical theologian in India.

1. Ecumenism as Testimony

M. M. Thomas speaks about his faith formation or theological formation as ecumenical formation through which he understands his Christian commitment and calling. In his book titled *My Ecumenical Journey*, Thomas defines ecumenism as testimony of a Christian who recognizes and realizes his or her calling to be the true disciple of the Christ crucified. He explains:

> Ecumenical formation is to take part in the world-wide fellowship of people committed to exploring the meaning of Christ and Church for our modern world and to building up a movement of Christian ecumenism as a spiritual support to the larger ecumenism struggling for human community (Thomas, 1990: 3).

As Thomas explains, ecumenical formation is closely connected to our theological formation and thus it becomes our testimony of faith. Christian faith is something that provokes us to seek the meaning of humanity in Christ and in Christian fellowship—the Church which is called and committed to the building up of a just community in this world. Christian faith is always communitarian and participatory. It seeks meaning in the participation of the struggles for fuller humanity which is ecumenical in content and practice. We become unecumenical when we define our faith as exclusive, private, and non-participatory. Fr. Sebastian Kappen defined Christian faith in terms of *gift* and *challenge*. Giftness of our faith explains its divine content and the challenge signifies the human part in it. Thus, for Kappen, theological formation is a *theandric practice* where we participate faithfully in the divine program of redemption of all (Kappen, 1993: 5). I am afraid, the concept of theological education as a faithful practice as well as an ecumenical practice has terribly been neglected in our context and thus we never experience a growth either in our faith formation or in our ecumenical thinking. This is one of the major challenges that theological education in India faces today.

2. Ecumenism as Open-Ecclesiology

Thomas argues for a radical ecclesiology as the basis of a genuine ecumenical formation in and through a meaningful theological education. According to Thomas, a closed Christian community in terms of its ethnicity, caste, and nationality is a fundamental flaw. A church that stands for its own rights and privileges in a multi-religious context nullifies its call and commission to be the church of the Christ crucified. A religious community that remains as an exclusive-theological community can never claim the status of a church. The Church becomes the community of love when it assumes a radical ontology of openness and inclusivity. The Church should be response-able and participatory in society. Thomas believes the true nature of the Church is of a body immersed in society.

The Church, for Thomas, exists in its mission. It exists in its participation for the building up of a just society. Thomas explains the features of the mission of the Church in India: (1) to resist the idolatry of power and wealth and other gods of death in India's collective life, (2) to be in solidarity with the poor and the oppressed in their struggle for justice, and (3) to give up communal self-interest and self-identity for the sake of creating in India a secular national community in the midst of India's religious and ideological pluralism, through manifesting a fellowship in Christ, transcending class, caste, ethnic and religious communal divisions (Thomas, 1990: 11). The question that we ask here is whether Indian Church has ever experienced the *koinonia* in Christ beyond its ethnic/

linguistic/gender/caste enclosures. It is here theological education in India realizes its tasks and responsibilities to inculcate an authentic ecumenical formation of inclusivity.

3. Ecumenism as Eschatological Humanism

Thomas' final goal of ecumenical formation is to be/come part of the New Humanity in Jesus Christ. Thomas understands history as the vibrant space of divine intervention. Salvation is not all ahistorical and apolitical. Salvation is nothing but humanization. Humanization is becoming a New Human in Christ which is eschatological in content. However, New Humanity is not a utopia that is to be achieved in the coming future; rather it is an immediate and local experience in Christ. It is inherent in the faith and practices of the believing community—the Church. The Church is an eschatological community that witnesses the coming age today. Alluding to the eschatological mission of the Church in India, Thomas writes:

> The Church in India is called to proclaim the gospel of the crucified and risen Christ as the source of redemption of all spiritualties underlying religion as well as ideologies, and to demonstrate the Koinonia in Christ around the Eucharist as the nucleus of a movement of the larger Koinonia in Christ uniting peoples of diverse religions, ideologies and cultures—as well as the cosmos with its bio-diversity (Thomas, 1995: 8).

For Thomas, Church is called to witness New Humanity in Jesus Christ, which is nothing but a secular koinonia in crucified Christ. According to Thomas, this New Humanity in Jesus Christ transforms Christianity, other religions, and other ideologies from within and envisages a radical secular koinonia which is based on the notion of a becoming humanism—eschatological humanism (Thomas, 1987: 119). The challenge before theological education in this manner is to envisage a dialogical, trans-disciplinary, and a secular platform where all agree with the crucial point—the eschatological humanism.

4. Theological Education in India: Challenges and Prospects

Having said the challenges in the ecumenical formation, let us think together to make our theological education more meaningful and relevant today. As we have already discussed, becoming ecumenical today is to uphold a participatory faith as testimony and make our Church an open-ended fellowship of all beyond the enclosures. Seeking for a common platform that goes beyond the religious, ideological, and theological boundaries is a strong criterion to re-make our ecumenical formation today. In this section, some pointers are suggested to reclaim the ecumenical content of our theological education in India today.

1. Faith as Theo-Politics

Let me share an experience that I have faced in one of my seminary classes on feminist theology. It was a discussion on the violence against women, specifically on rape victims. Neglecting my passion and sensitivity on the issue, a few students seemed indifferent in the class. I asked them the reason. They said: "Sir, don't you know about the counselling tips for the rape victims? Now healing process of the rape victims has become easier and simple than ever. Then why should we worry about it?" Does our theological education make our budding theologians insensitive, impassionate and oblivious? Does our theological education lose its critical edge and become apolitical in content? Does our theological education fail to translate the meaning of Christian faith in its participation of struggles of the marginalized and the victims of the oppressions? If then, what kind of transformation does our theological education have to envision today to make our Church and theological academy politically sensitive?

Mark Lewis Taylor speaks about two types of theologies: one is 'guild theology', which is formulated in the 'ghettoized communities.' This guild theology, according to Taylor, is founded on the 'ethos of transcendence', which helps this theology to be insensitive and apolitical while talking about universal salvation. Second is the *theo-politics* which always seeks the meaning of faith in participation of the agonistic politics of the crucified bodies of this world (Taylor,

2011: xi). Which of these epistemological foundations design our theological formation today?

2. Church as a Messianic Community

Once I asked my theological students to prepare some Bible studies from a Dalit context. The Interesting thing was that all students prepared their Bible studies from the same texts: Samaritan woman, Slave girl, Haemorrhaged woman, Syrophoenician woman, etc. Why it is so? Why are other Biblical stories not conducive for Dalit context? This is called hermeneutical essentialism. Essentialization is the political process of fixing categories and peoples into closed ontologies. In Indian theological academia, it more or less happens with the lives of marginalized sections. The problem with this type of hermeneutics is the fixation of the subaltern life-world, which is always multi-faceted, multi-colored and polyphonic. Only a messianic hermeneutics can affirm the 'irreducible singularity' of 'the other' and allow the other to retain either agency and alterity.

Church as a messianic community always re-imagines itself beyond the enclosures and fixities and envisions itself as a community to come. Indian theological education is to be critically analyzed in the sense of how far it has been successful to inculcate the logic of a coming community in India where we all are divided in terms of caste, gender, and ethnicity, how far we are able to transcend divisions and become ecumenical in life and witness in this country. There is a great task that is waiting for Indian theological education in the process of making the Church a coming community.

3. Polydoxy as Theological Methodology

M. M. Thomas' focus on a trans-disciplinary methodology to envisage a secular koinonia in Christ today necessitates a polydoxical methodology through which theology overcomes the binaries of secular/sacred, religion/politics, theism/atheism, spirit and matter, God and the world. It was Catherine Keller and Laurel C. Schneider who proposed this term to re-signify theological paradigms in the contemporary context. For them, theology in the contemporary context would uphold a "rhizomatic radicality" which is founded on a "polydoxic" philosophical/theoretical/religious inheritance. Keller contends that "such "rhizomatic radicality" is not about uprooting our traditions but about exposing them to our confounding togetherness—as species, peoples, genders, sexualities, races, religions, even—Lord help us—our Christianities" (Kaputo & Keller, 2007: 108). The Christianity, not only Christian Theology, is invited here to validate the multiplicity of its being, becoming, and belonging on this planet earth.

In fact, this polydoxical methodology is not new in India. Kiran Sebastian has offered a discussion on this issue of trans-disciplinarity in Indian theological education years before, but had not received much attention as such. Kiran wrote an article on the topic—"Can We Now Bypass That Truth'—Interrogating the Methodology of Dalit Theology," and sought a polydoxical platform for theological articulation in India by taking Dalit theology as a case. He writes:

> Dalit theology, which at one stage was accused of being a narrow theological 'ism', of relevance only to those who had the 'pathos' experiences, or were in empathetic or sympathetic agreement with it, draws its strength from the rich and complex inter-connections with the methodological possibilities thrown up by epistemological inquiry in the spectrum of fields of knowledge. In other words, the strength of Dalit theology lies precisely in the possibility of its inter-disciplinarity, something that needs to be acknowledged and fostered (Sebastian: 2008).

Taking polydoxy as methodology, Dalit theology brings the epistemological dialogue between Indian materialist philosophy and Christian philosophy; Ambedkar's neo-Buddhism and Christian theology; atheism and theism; religion and politics, etc. It is an invocation to unearth the indigenous epistemological traditions and bring it in dialogue with the Christian philosophy for envisaging an ethico-political community of love and justice in and around us.

Conclusion

Theological education in India needs to take the turns to theo-politics, eschatological ecclesiology and Polydoxical methodology for re-signifying the Indian Church and Ecumenical Movement to be relevant and meaningful today. It is to be started with the theological academy so that it may be reflected in the life and witness of the Church in India. Theological academy has a vital role to play outside of the Church to envisage an eschatological humanism for all. For that matter, modules should be re-drafted and syllabi should be re-articulated. The participatory content of the learning process is to be highlighted so that the candidates may get enough opportunities to feel the agonistic politics of the marginalized. The basic quality that we expect from a theologian is nothing but the humility to journey with the 'other' to the unknown, not to 'eat out the other'; but to get transformed by the 'other' as we see in the life and witness of M. M. Thomas.

References

John D. Caputo and Catherine Keller, *Crosscurrents*, Winter 2007, 105-11 at 108.

Kiran Sebastian, "Can We Now Bypass That Truth'—Interrogating the Methodology of Dalit Theology," in *Revisiting and Resignifying Methodology for Dalit Theology*, edited by James Massey and Indukur Mohan Razu (New Delhi & Bangalore: CDS & UTC, 2008).

Mark Lewis Taylor, *The Theological and the Political: On the Weight of the World* (Minneapolis: Fortress Press, 2011).

M. M. Thomas, *My Ecumenical Journey 1947-1975* (Trivandrum: Ecumenical Publishing Center Private Limited, 1990).

M. M. Thomas, "The Church in India—Witness to the Meaning of the Cross Today," in *Future of the Church in India*, ed., Aruna Gnanadason (Nagpur: NCCI, 1990).

M. M. Thomas, *A Diaconal Approach to Indian Ecclesiology* (Rome & Tiruvalla: CIIS & CSS, 1995).

M. M. Thomas, *Risking Christ for Christ's Sake: Towards an Ecumenical Theology of Pluralism* (Geneva: WCC Publications, 1987).

Sebastian Kappen, "Towards an Indian Theology of Liberation," *Readings in Indian Christian Theology*, edited by R.S. Sugirtharajah and Cecil Hargreaves (Delhi: ISPCK, 1993).

13

Mission Re-defined: Voices from the Margins*

Margins are a strange window to the world; they offer to sight a perspective into the everyday even while luring the gaze to a different world that defies the visualization. And precisely because of these reasons they are dangerous: they bring to sight what should not be revealed and entertain visions unsettling to the order of things.

(Vitor Westhelle, 2010: 122)

Introduction

Margin is often defined as the site of weakness and vulnerability. It is located at the periphery, but is tempting to move to the centre. As the site of peripherality, the margin is always in need of empowerment.

* Paper presented at the National Conference on Mission at Dharma Jyoti Vidya Peeth, Faridabad on 23-25 February, 2017.

Christian mission, as a project of empowerment and emancipation, found the marginalized as the site of its redemptive engagement in modern history. However, no one can deny the contributions of the modern missionary movements for the upliftment of the marginalized communities over the globe. Whether it is in Africa, Asia or Latin America, the missionary impact in the emancipation of the marginalized sections in the South can never be neglected or rejected.

However, the contemporary paradigm shifts in the epistemology and methodology demand new readings of the mission archives and the positioning of the 'missionized' in the mission histories. The postcolonial studies help us to relocate the position of marginality as the site of postcoloniality where the margin is de-marginalized and the centre is de-centered. Christian mission narratives in the postcolonial re-reading necessitate a deconstructive look into the mission archives in order to 'redeem' the voices from the margins. The redeemed voices of the margins speak about new mission engagements of mutuality and envision the multiple spaces of negotiation between the missionary and the missionized so that Christian mission in the postcolonial context could not be the oxymoron.

1. Re-defining Margin: Methodological Contentions

While exposing the positionality of the slave bodies in the European colonial narratives, Achille Mbembe, the African philosopher and thinker talks about a term called 'thing'—that is something that somewhere is *nothing* (Mbembe, 2001: 3). Mbembe further defines margin as a 'thing' that 'possesses life, property, and body as if they were alien things' (Mbembe, 2001: 187). Here, the margin is an *invention* (Mudimbe, 1988), an *idea* (Mudimbe, 1994), and an imagined myth of the colonizer. Margin is considered here as a fixed/essentialized space that can be easily conquered or accommodated within the colonial project. Mbembe finds fecundity in postcolonial methodology to re-position the *thing* into *something*, the object into subject, the silenced into actor, the colonized into decolonized. Postcoloniality is to envisage the margin as the postcolonial subject who upholds the agency and the right to be different (alterity).

Postcoloniality, for Mbembe, is the rhetorical space where the colonial subject becomes the postcolonial subject by repudiating the embodied colonialism from within. According to Mbembe, the postcolonial methodology overcomes the limitation of the subaltern methodology as it tried to re-present the margins as fixed/ essentialized figures (Spivak, 2008: 19). Margin as postcoloniality is the rhetorical space where the silenced speaks and the other becomes de-othered. In that sense, as Vitor Westhelle rightly said, "Margins are a strange window to the world that has a 'disturbing revelatory potential' to redraft our own visualizations and our gazes upon the 'others' "(Westhelle, 2010: 122). Here margins become the sites of transfiguration and thereby denis their fixed figurations as the 'colonial invention'/ 'discovery'/ 'idea.' Margin, in postcolonial methodology, occupies a fluid space that makes its representation im/possible.

How do we listen to the voice of the margin which never speaks or cannot be heard in the colonial institutional structures? To listen to the silenced/muted, we need special training. Gayatri Chakravorty Spivak calls it *the training in the imagination*—the training to listen to the ghost speaking. Spivak calls it the training in the process of *teleopoiesis. Teleopoiesis* is a training to listen to the other by de-essentializing the other. The other here is not at all a fixed figure but a transfigured figure. It is a radical pedagogy of knowing—knowing the other, listening to the mute, listening to the ghost. The Derridean term *teleopoiesis* is used here by Spivak to signify the process of creating toward an ever-distant future (a-venir) in terms of time. Spivak, on the other hand, defines it as creating a distant future with a 'distant other.' It suggests that there is an unbridgeable gap between the self and the other. The other, as ghost, is a mystery. the other is always enigmatic and alluric. Figuring the other is as impossible as bottling thunder! The other is beyond our comprehension. *Teleopoiesis* upholds the 'irreducible singularity'— the incomprehensibility of the other.

According to Spivak, *teleopoiesis* demands a turning off of the self's voice. She defines it as an embrace of a different episteme— "deconstructive embrace" —which requires the suspension of the hegemonic language and the institutional practices that cauterize the other. There are two dimensions to this pedagogy; one is to "learn to learn from the (subordinated) other," which is nothing but a "self-suspending leap into other's sea" (Simmons). The second dimension is to "learn to unlearn one's privileges." Spivak says: "Our privileges, whatever they be in terms of race, class, nationality, gender and the like, may have prevented us from gaining a certain kind of Other knowledge" (Spivak, 1998: 4). Spivak argues, that it requires an education that re-orients our thinking of ourselves and knowing of the other. We need to learn to learn to the other. Here, the other is conceived not as an absolutely exterior other, rather; it is a relational one that helps us to deconstruct our own self-knowledge. *Teleopoiesis* as the postcolonial methodology offers a deconstructive practice to train ourselves to listen to the voices from the margin. Thus, the postcolonial approach helps us to problematize our own epistemological locations and enable us to re-constitute it on the basis of the *deconstructive embrace*.

2. Re-defining Mission: Margins as Potential Site of Transfigurations

In the process of redeeming the voices of the margins from the modern mission archives and re-positiong the postcolonial subjects as the agents of Christian mission, the postcolonial mission studies offer us various significant models of doing mission today.

2.1. Mode of Mutuality

Chad M. Bauman, in his study on Dalit women converts in colonial North India in the early nineteenth century, problematizes the claim of the Western Feminists who argue that the subaltern women had exercised their agency (Bauman, 2008: 5-27). Bauman argues that Dalit women who converted to Christianity often experienced a contraction of the range of their activities (Bauman, 2008: 27). In the same vein of thought, Jane Haggis, in her study on the Bible Women in Travancore South India offers us a postcolonial methodology of redeeming subaltern women voices from the colonial mission narratives (Haggis, 2000: 81-113). According to Haggis, the "mission of sisterhood" as it was conceived by the Western missionary wives to convert indigenous women to "good wives and mothers" was an occasion for the 'native women' to empower themselves in a complex context of caste and gender rather than being subjects of, mediums for, the emancipatory goals of the mission" (Haggis, 2000: 106-7).

Mrinalini Sebastian analyzes that the indigenous Bible women exercised a 'negotiated agency' in-between the missionary wives and the native women (Sebastian, 2003: 5-3). Taking the cue from Mrinalini Sebastian, Gladson Jathanna, on the other hand, argues that there was 'a mode of mutuality' between the missionary women and the native Bible women through which they both achieved "a new mode of understanding one's own self, never without one's other, not at the centre but in the margins" (Jathanna, 2015: 145). Jathanna finds the postcolonial space of the mission in-between where the silenced women, irrespective of their racial/geographical differences, speaking/walking/praying/singing/learning together. Highlighting the feminine face of the Christian mission, Jathanna affirms: "Their [native Bible women] voices, though feeble in tone, affirm Christian faith beyond the well-established dogmatic frameworks of the mission agency and the Church" (Jathanna, 2015: 146). For Jathanna, the mode of mutuality in mission as we see in the story of the native Bible women, is the postcolonial space of negotiating subjectivity through which both native women and missionary women tried to re-articulate themselves. He writes: "They stood, walked, sang, laughed, cried and lived in a mutual relationship where they negotiated a defined and designed subjectivity and demanded a mutual subjectivity." (Jathanna, 2006: 137).

2.2. Reclaiming the Liberative Difference

Based on the African womanist theologians' study on the issues of Sex, Stigma, and HIV/AIDS in African women, Letty M. Russel offers a method of reclaiming the difference as the gift of God to re-imagine mission in the postcolonial world. In the postcolonial context, difference cannot be considered as the site of domination and subordination, but it has a liberatory potential in our lives. Russel quotes Audre Lorde to make her argument clear:

> ...it is not the differences between us that are separating us. It is rather our refusal to recognize those differences, and to examine the distortions which result from our misnaming them and their effects upon human behavior and expectations (Lorde, 1984: 115).

According to Russel, the essentialization of marginality makes it possible to use it as a structural weapon of oppression. Essentialization of marginality declares that the differences of race, sex, class and sexual orientation are part of created nature and cannot be changed. On this basis, it is possible to justify oppression, poverty, exploitation and imperialism by declaring that the dominating group has been created to rule the world. On the other hand, Russel argues, the reclaiming of liberative difference demands the building up of relational differences. Liberative difference offers space for alterity—the freedom to define itself —yet recognizing the interconnectivity and conviviality. It can be done through forming coalitions across the difference. Liberative difference as the postcolonial methodological mission approach, the African women despite their differences find a platform together along with their Anglo European women friends to resist the death-dealing stigma of HIV/AIDS. Of course, the liberative difference approach requires the development of networks that can sustain groups in their struggles, and provide opportunities for partnership as postcolonial subjects. It is to become people who "put their bodies on the line as living sacrifices (Rom 12: 1-2) and to be aware of the surrounding 'cloud of witnesses" (Heb. 12: 1).

What we see in the mode of mutuality is the possibility of a negotiated subjectivity in the mission engagement, while we find the possibility of the margin to envisage a common mission to fight against the social evils that distort the human subjectivities. By de-essentializing the margin, their agency is affirmed and celebrated in a mode of deconstructive embrace. This is the way we de-margin the margin and de-other the other. Only through *teleopoiesis*—'turning off one's own voice and leaping into the other's sea' we are able to experience the 'mode of mutuality' and 'the liberative difference.' When the *teleopoiesis* actualizes mutuality and liberative difference, the margin becomes the site of transfiguration of bodies—

transfiguration of natural bodies into spiritual bodies (1 Cori. 15:40). Thus, Margin is a site of revelatory space of multiplicity and manyness where the mission of God and the God of mission are re-imagined and re-constituted for the sake of mission itself.

3. Mission Re-defined: Theological Underpinnings

How do we re-imagine a theology of mission in the postcolonial context where the margins become the potential site of transfiguration? Christian mission, as a modern Western theological concept founded on the concept of Great Commission that gives (Western) Church legitimacy and power, needs to be decolonized in the contemporary postcolonial context in order to envisage a mission in the margins. Mission as the mode of mutuality and the liberative difference in fact interrogate the 'closed ecclesiologies' that fixes its 'missiological/ soteriological other' outside of its ontology. The modern missiological concepts such as 'reaching out,' 'mission field,' 'mission to HIV/AIDS' etc. problematizes those 'closed ecclesiologies' and necessitates new imaginations of *ekklesia* as the coming community. Called to live between the Church in the world and the Church that comes, *ekklesia* is a becoming/belonging community in the making. It is here our ecclesiological thinking is invoked to de-imperialize the Church in terms of power and hierarchy and to become the Church of the multitude. In order to de-imperialize the Church, Giorgio Agamben asks the Church to return to its messianic vocation to become the Church in the margins—a community of the people who have no community at all (Agamben: 2013).

Anne Joh, the Asian-American Christian theologian, offers us a theology of the crucified God who finds the cross as the experience of the margin. Alluding to the concept of the abject (Judith Butler) as the experience of the crucified in-between the objectification and the subject formation envisages a potential space of salvation. Here God is not conceived as the sovereign God who discharges salvation to the margin from outside; rather it is a God, Jesus Christ, who embodies the salvation in his experiences of torture and pain. God of the margin doesn't discharge salvation from outside while upholding the sovereignty intact. On the other way around, it is a God who ceases to be sovereign and omnipotent and becoming the potential body of salvation for the tortured and marginalized in the world on the cross. The Christian God of the modern mission has to be re-imagined as the crucified God—the one who in-operates the sovereign power within and becomes God-self the weak and the vulnerable.

Theology of mission in the postcolonial context has to be theopolitic in content as it embodies the agonies and the anxieties of the marginalized. Margin as the site of the transfiguration evokes a life in common–where all enjoy the commonwealth of the public. Margin as the rhetorical space of postcoloniality always cherishes a democracy of the weak that always resists any kind of political, economic and cultural imperialism. In short, Christian mission in the postcolonial context does not become the oxymoron, but become the hope of the marginalized, who always seek for the mode of mutuality and liberative difference within, and thereby they become the 'localized' site of the salvation for all. Mission in the margin witnesses the fragments of salvation; rather than the one and only universal salvation. Christian mission is an invitation to embody the experiences of salvation which is offered to the margin—a complex site of resistance and celebration. It is here the Church becomes a coming community and its liturgy becomes the politics of transfiguration.

References

Achille Mbembe, *On the Postcolony* (Berkley: University of California Press, 2001).

Audre Lorde, *Sister Outsider: Essays and Speeches* (NY: The Crossing Press, 1984).

Chad m. Bauman, "Redeeming Indian 'Christian' Womanhood?: Missionaries, Dalits, and Agency in Colonial India," *Journal of Feminist Studies in Religion* 24:2 (2008), 5-27.

Giorgio Agamben, *The Church and The Kingdom* (London & New York: Seagull, 2013).

Gladson Jathanna, *Mode of Mutuality in the Margins of Mission: Hermannsburg Women's Mission in India* (Bangalore: Dharmaram Publications, 2015).

Jane Haggis, "'Good wives and mothers' or 'dedicated workers'? Contradictions of domesticity in the 'mission of sisterhood', Travancore, South India," in *Maternities and Modernities: Colonial and Postcolonial Experiences in Asia and the Pacific*, edited by Kalpana Ram and Margaret Jolly (Cambridge: Cambridge University Press, 2000), 81-113.

Mrinalini Sebastian, "Reading Archives from a Postcolonial Feminist Perspective: "Native" Bible Women and the Missionary Ideal," in *Journal of Feminist Studies in Religion*, Vol. 19, No.1 (Spring, 2003), pp 5-25.

Spivak, *Other Asias* (Oxford: Blackwell, 2008).

Spivak, *The Spivak Reader: Selected Work of Gayatri Chakravorty Spivak,* Donna Landry and Gerald M. Maclean eds., (New York & Routledge, 1998).

Valentin Mudimbe, *The Invention of Africa: Gnosis, Philosophy and the Order of Knowledge* (Indianapolis: Indiana University Press, 1988).

Y. T. Vinayaraj, *Intercessions* (Delhi: ISPCK, 2016).

Vitor Westhelle, *After Heresy: Colonial Practices and Post-colonial Theologies* (Oregon: Cascade Books, 2010).